# Tucked Up in Bed

by

## Jennie Rayment

# Acknowledgements

This book is once more dedicated to Nick Diment without whose unfailing help, support, advice and encouragement, none of this would ever have happened. He has tolerated tantrums, tears and distress, jollied me along and administered a good kick (metaphorically) when necessary. Marvellous man! He, now copes with me in permanent residence - must be mad!

A very special thank you must be given to Basil Crisp who, yet again, has waded through all my ill-written proofs, messy punctuation and howling grammatical whoppers, and still speaks to me! I am very grateful to Patsy Yardley for volunteering to check the proofs, her advice has been so valuable in the past and I am delighted that she has offered to help with the third book. In addition, my thanks are extended to Stephen Smith, the printer and Aaron (his son), who have both come up trumps; and Nick Diment, the photographer, for coping with all the photographs, and Raymond Reid of Haslemere for their help with developing the films.

Also, my thanks and gratitude to Midge Pitter, Jean Collett, Joan Ryan, Joan Sortwell and Peggy and Joan Douglas, who not only loaned their work for photography but offered to test the techniques. Shelagh Jarvis has again been of amazing help; she made two of the quilts and proof read the words, I can't thank her enough. Smashing lady with a super husband. Pam Balls deserves a mention because she has always had faith in me, Lynette Harris because she has been so helpful and Milo as she suggested the idea for the cover. Once more, a further thank you must be extended to all the students who have borne with fortitude my teaching, listened to my lectures, laughed and giggled with me, and who still come back for more. A further big thank you must be extended to the Bishops - both Tom and Diana were extremely helpful. Not only did they lend their beautiful bed for the photographs but Tom loaned his body, forgot his principles and climbed into bed with me. Finally, a thank you to all my family, especially my son without whom none of this would ever have happened, but one of us has to keep him!

Copyright © Jennie Rayment 1998          ISBN 0-9524675-1-8
First Published February 1999 by J.R. Publications
5 Queen Street, Emsworth,
Hampshire, PO10 7BJ.   Tel/Fax: 01243 374860 E-mail jenrayment@aol.com

Printed by St. Richard's Press Limited
Leigh Road, Terminus Industrial Estate,
Chichester, West Sussex PO19 2TU.
Tel: 01243 782988

# Contents

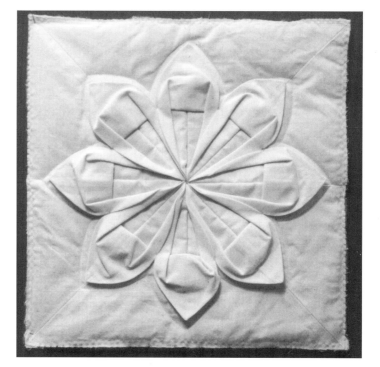

# Tucked Up in Bed

This is intended to be a light-hearted tome devoted to 'Nipping and Tucking'. It contains even more new and fascinating methods of twiddling fabric to create a further abundance of convoluted shapes. As ever all the ideas are fundamentally simple but can be manipulated to your heart's desire.

Quiltmaking is the ultimate aim of all these devious machinations and the underlying theme discusses the creation of a sampler quilt. **'Tucked Up in Bed'** presents twelve individual and innovative designs in addition to relevant information on basic construction technique. In addition, other projects from **'Tucks Textures & Pleats'** and **'Tucks & Textures Two'** (previous books by the author on fabric manipulation) are mentioned briefly and the exact measurements for making these designs are given. Novel schemes for borders and layout are included with lots of hints, tips and useful suggestions scattered throughout the text. There can be nothing nicer than waking up in the morning underneath a warm quilt, snuggled up to your loved one or, as I often used to be, curled round the last night's cup of cold coffee, with glasses (still on nose) and yesterday's crossword puzzle. Of course you don't have to make a quilt - there's no reason why the designs cannot be used for cushions, bags, boxes, table-linen and wall-hangings etc. or indeed any other item you fancy.

In addition, to provide a little light relief, various anecdotes are tucked into the chapters covering a variety of subjects from tales of travel to seamy stories of steamy sex!! Incidentally, for those who have read the previous books, I am reverting to the original style of **'Tucks Textures & Pleats'** in having innumerable exclamation marks. Furthermore some dreadful English phraseology, tautology and absolutely awful alliteration is included for which I make no apology!

Apropos the seamy stories, I am becoming rapidly aware that I extol the virtues of 'Nipping, Tucking, Stuffing, Rolling, Twiddling and Fiddling' at great length but most of the time this is related to material. In addition, one of my lecture topics features 'The Muslin Mistress' and during the lecture I remove some but not all of my clothing. Consequently I feel that I should justify both this title and my reputation for a little stuffing and expand upon the theme! I don't believe that there are any stitching manuals that ever mention sex or even just the opposite sex: so read on - this particular literary edifice may surprise you.

The greatest influence behind my writing has always been the chief cook, bottle washer and proof reader in my life - a Mr. Diment. I met this gentleman through the columns of 'The Times' newspaper and apart from the similarity of our names (no quips about being 'ment' for one another) we have discovered various other mutually agreeable attributes. Anyway to cut a long story short I felt that it may add a touch of spice to **'Tucked Up in Bed'** to relate one or two of the adventures that happened along the way.

*But do not fret there is nothing to be ashamed of - it's all terribly British and stiff upper lip and all that.*

Before I begin here is a short description of the author and her work taken from an American publicity leaflet:-

*'Jennie Rayment is a skinnyish, red-haired, slightly wacky Brit who is totally obsessed with 'Nipping and Tucking' - fabric manipulation and surface texture. She is known as the 'Calico Queen' in Britain or the 'Muslin Mistress'\* in the USA as the majority of her work is made from unbleached cotton material (calico in England - muslin in America). Nowadays she is becoming internationally known for her quick, simple, innovative techniques with manipulated material. Prior to this she taught Patchwork and Quilting to both recreational classes and for the City & Guild Examination courses, obtained her teaching diploma and became an official verifier/assessor for City & Guild Patchwork Examinations. Her work has been exhibited in numerous galleries and at national shows and exhibitions; she has written various articles for both magazines and books.*

*Suddenly her life changed - she became disenchanted with matching points in her patchwork, fretting over which colours to use and having to press everything flat. She wanted to ruffle the surface! Now she manipulates, tucks, pleats, folds, twiddles and stuffs her fabric shapes to produce some fascinating and innovative designs. Diving into these ingenuous creations, she wrote the book **'Tucks Textures & Pleats'** packed with natty notions for textured topics, which was followed by **'Tucks and Textures Two'** containing even more possibilities for surface manipulation. The nicest thing about all these ideas is that they are basically very easy; can be adapted for any types of material; can be made any size and used anywhere. From Patchworkers to Embroiderers, Interior Designers and Fashion students, in fact anyone who likes playing with fabrics can obtain many creative ideas from her magic manipulations. There is no need to own a fancy sewing machine - all the effects can be made by anyone using any machine from a hand/treadle to the latest singing and dancing techno-computerised model; you can do everything by hand but it takes a month of Sundays!! No experience is necessary and the only skill required is the ability to thread a needle and possibly sew a straightish line. Her creations are fast, fun and appealing and can be used for all kinds of items from cushions, quilts, wall-hangings, boxes, baskets, table linen and of course fashion garments. She has just returned from a long tour of the States and is off again to New Zealand and will be persuading them to "Nip and Tuck". So from the 'Bias Bobble' to the 'Origami Twist' (done to music!), scrunching, ruching, interweaving, interlocking, folding, twiddling and squashing, there are some really fantastic textured effects.'*

\* Just why do they call me the 'Muslin Mistress'? Those of you who have read the second book may remember the anecdote (page 95) relating the tale of my son modelling at the 'Walkabout Wearables Luncheon' in Houston. He was the star of the show and what an act to follow! To make an impact at the next year's show, I decided to go as the 'Muslin Mistress'. The outfit consists of a frilly brolly (umbrella), Pilgrim's Scrip bag, scrunchy, ruched and beaded hat, tucked-up vest or waistcoat (USAspeak versus Britspeak), a shirt with many holes revealing various areas of naked flesh, a textured skirt embellished with stuffed 'Trumpets' and a pair of flounced and beribboned bloomers! This entire ensemble makes me look like a well stuffed pixie!! So we prance around the stage and the high point of the show is to ......... That you will have to imagine!!!

# Creating a Sampler Quilt

## What is a Sampler Quilt?

A collection of differently patterned pieces that are stitched together to form a larger piece of work as in the photograph. The pieces or blocks as they are usually termed are normally square and of equal size. Frequently the blocks are separated by bands of material called **sashing**. These **sashing** bands border each of the pieces and make a framework that connects the designs together. Plain strips of fabric could be used as the connecting sections or they can be constructed from a series of individual pieces stitched together, thus creating further opportunities for supplementary patterns.

There is no reason why all the blocks have to be different and sometimes it is preferable to have a repeat of certain designs to produce some form of cohesion to the overall appearance.

In the majority of sampler quilts, the blocks themselves are created by some form of a distinct pattern within the square unit, with all non-patterned spaces forming the background to the motif. Frequently the internal design is symmetrical, and in the main the pattern is *two dimensional*. There are thousands of different patterns originating from all over the world. Many of them are combinations of geometric shapes and are pieced together (stitched), but there are hundreds that have a set arrangement of shapes applied to the background material. Most of them are named but the names can vary from one country to another.

'**Tucked Up in Bed**' uses this basic format but all the blocks are *three dimensional*. Some of the designs in this book have their origins based on traditional design but some of them are new, or so I hope. Sadly there is nothing really innovative in this world - very probably someone somewhere has thought of the same idea before but I have not yet seen these particular creations made up.

The nicest thing about constructing a sampler quilt or even just making one block is that you can personalise it. **You** can choose the colours, the fabrics and, in the case of these designs, whether you manipulate and twiddle a little more or just stay with the basic shape. Once you start fiddling with the pieces then there is no end to the possibilities.

# Designing and Making a Sampler Quilt

*Who says you have to make a quilt?* The completed blocks can always be turned into cushions, bags, table-mats or small wall-hangings. We are all very good at being fired with enthusiasm to make a specific project, then it fizzles out and we are left with yet another lot of UFO's (UnFinished Objects), although some of us are dedicated enough to complete the chosen task.

## What Kind?

Assuming that you are setting out to make a quilt, the next decision is which one? Do not forget that there are many types from pram, cot, lap, single, double, queen and king-sized - you do not have to make a king-sized but could always stop at a pram-sized one! This could be just one block with a border or two to make it a little bigger, and you would still learn basic quilt making techniques. If this is your first quilt then start small - remember that from tiny acorns, mighty oaks might grow!

## How Big?

In an ideal world everyone would plan the quilt, draw a scale model of the ultimate design, then make it up. This is very difficult if you have never made a quilt and have no real understanding of the basic construction. Before you start you should decide on the approximate finished size; but this doesn't always happen and one constructs an assortment of squares with no final plan in view. My advice to those 'first-timers' would be to decide on the approximate completed size. As you are creating a series of squares that will probably be linked together with sashing (borders), the ultimate size of the quilt can be adjusted by the width of these bands - wide bands = larger quilt; narrow bands = smaller quilt. In addition the quilt will probably have borders round the outer edge to frame the central design and these can vary in width, quantity and pattern. It's amazing how many borders can be attached when a too small piece needs to be increased to fit a specific space.

## How Many Blocks?

In my opinion constructing 9, 15, 25 or 35 blocks is preferable. These specific quantities when stitched together all have a central square. Quilts do look better if the design has a specific focus, and as you'll probably commence with no definite conception of the end result, the opportunity to identify one particular block for the centre is most useful. The remainder of the blocks can be then be arranged in a pleasing format.

As you *near the completion of block-making,* I suggest that you *lay out the quilt blocks* to get the general impression so far. This allows you to get a rough overview of the final appearance and make any remaining blocks to complement the existing ones. Should you find that there is any glaring misjudgement in your proposed layout now is the time to change it. After all you could always make a different block to replace it. Panic not if you forget to do this, as even the biggest 'jumble' of multifarious colours, shapes and patterns will look pleasing when sashed. These bands create a framework and provide an overall uniformity and cohesion to the design.

All the *measurements* of the following examples are calculated on the accurate *finished sizes* and assuming that you have seamed all the pieces correctly.

## Cot and Pram Quilts

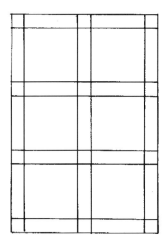

The sizes for these vary tremendously and I would advise checking the specific measurements before you begin. It may not be possible to have the blocks arranged with a central square and *four or six 12"(30cm) squares* may be sufficient. Increase to the correct size with the addition of sashing and/or borders. Think carefully about the suitability of the blocks chosen: too many folds and twiddly bits could be difficult to launder and small fingers may catch in the folds. I would strongly recommend that all the materials are washed initially in a mild soap solution to remove any harmful chemicals in the fibres.

## Lap Quilts, Small Wall-hangings & Quillows
*(Quilt that turns into a pillow)*

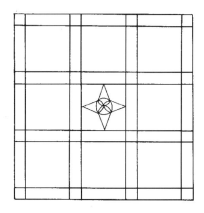

*Nine 12"(30cm)* squares stitched together without any sashing would form a *36"(90cm) square*; adding *3"(8cm)* strips of sashing will increase the size to *48"(122cm)* square. In addition, a block of nine squares (nine patch) has the advantageous feature of a central square. This can be used to create a specific focal point to the overall design.

## Bed Quilts

As mentioned previously there are several different standard sizes of beds. The majority of beds measure 75"(190cm) in length but the widths can alter. The other conundrum is the amount of bedding and pillows, plus the design of the bed. It is well worth measuring the complete bed over all the blankets, duvets etc., then decide how far the quilt should drop over the sides. I like to see the mattress covered and the quilt hanging slightly over the valance. If the quilt hangs too far down the sides then the corners will lie on the floor; resolve this problem by rounding the corners off (a real pain to construct) or use Shelagh Jarvis' tip and design the quilt with the corner blocks omitted. The final measurements and shape required will be your own decision. If you find the sheer size daunting, why not make a quilt to fit the top of the bed only?

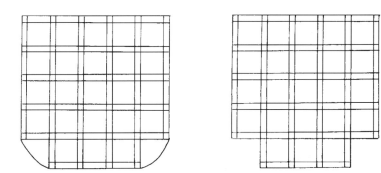

Most bed quilts will be rectangular rather than square which may create problems with the total design. Personally I prefer to have the main part of the sampler quilt actually on the bed with the framework of borders (plain or decorative) covering the sides.

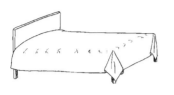

Normally, the quilt will drop over only three sides of the bed - this means that this extra length (drop) has to be added to those relevant edges. The top end of the quilt (by the headboard) may not always need any extension. It is a good idea to try the unfinished main quilt section in place before you attach any extra pieces.

One very important thing to mention is the *shrinkage caused by quilting - some allowance should be made in the initial measurements*. Once the quilt top has been completed then it will be layered with some form of batting/wadding and a backing material. These layers will be anchored together (quilted), usually with some type of stitchery. A certain degree of shrinking can occur depending on the amount and type of stitching done. Up to 2"- 3"(5cm - 7.5cm) may be lost overall, but this can be rectified by increasing the size of the final binding.

## Single Quilts

*Fifteen 12"(30cm) blocks* would be a useful quantity to make. If you joined all the blocks together the minimum dimensions would be *36"(90cm) x 60"(150cm)*. Adding *3"(8cm)* sashing bands will increase the size to *48"(122cm) x 78"(198cm)*. This will fit the top of most single beds but you may find a border or two necessary to cover all the bedding. An arrangement of fifteen squares has the added advantage of a central square as the linchpin of the composition as shown in left-hand drawing below.

## Double and Queen-sized Beds

A double bed is usually 54"(138cm) wide x 75"(190cm) long and the queen size is 60"(150cm) x 75"(190cm) length. *Twenty-five 12"(30cm) blocks* will be large enough to fit the width of both beds (right-hand diagram below). These do not have to be all different and a pleasing design can be made by repeating some of the blocks especially on the corners.

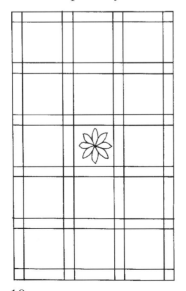

Use the centre block as the focus for your innovative layout. Purely stitching the blocks together will give a minimum measurement of _60" x 60"(150cm x 150cm)_ square. Adding _3"(8cm)_ sashing will increase the size to _78" x 78"(198cm x 198cm)_. Additional borders will be needed if the Quilt is to drop over any valance and/or cover the bedding. Do measure the bed carefully so that any extra dimensions may be calculated correctly.

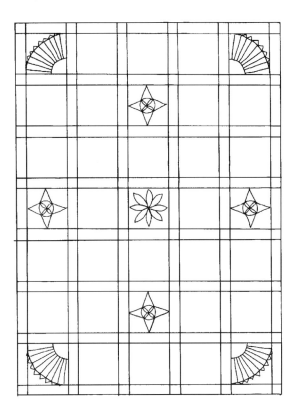

### King-sized Beds

Sit down quickly - a mere _thirty-five 12"(30cm) blocks_ may be necessary. (King-sized beds are usually _72"(180cm) wide x 75"(190cm)_ long.) The minimum dimensions of thirty-five blocks would be _60"(78cm) x 84"(108cm)_ if stitched solely together; with sashing attached the measurements would expand to _78"(198cm) x 108"(274cm)_. Use the centre square as a dynamic feature of the overall design. Once again, do measure the bed carefully so that any extra dimensions may be calculated correctly.

## Choice of Fabric?

Any natural fibre cloth may be used (natural fibres are easier to manipulate), and cotton is probably the best choice for beginners. There is no reason why silk cannot be incorporated but I would strongly suggest that the choice of material is pure cotton if this is your first attempt at quilt making. The man-made fibres do not take a crease well which can cause problems with the trickier manipulations.

You could always experiment with other kinds of fabric from chintz (glazed cotton), satin, denim, sateen, thin suedes or leathers, cretonnes and silk. The glazing of chintz reflects the shadows of any texture very well and can sometimes resemble a fine leather. If you select a fine silk add a little more 'body' to the fibres and prevent the fraying by ironing one of the fusible interfacings to the back. Fabric which creases well is useful when manipulating the surface, so try spray starching thinner materials such as lawn (fine smooth cotton cloth with a polished finish) to add extra crispness. Why not explore the use of cloth with a textured weave, patterned fabric and directional designs? Stripes really lend themselves to surface manipulation as you can play with the lines to add a further dimension to the design. Experiment with pre-textured material to enhance the desired creation.

As on so many previous occasions, I am using **calico** (unbleached cotton material) for many of the examples. **In the <u>USA</u> this particular cloth is referred to as <u>MUSLIN</u>**. One reason for selecting this type of fabric is the price. Calico is not expensive compared to other materials, consequently you can make vast piles of samples, explore, experiment and expand ideas without spending lots of money. In addition, the pale colour of the material reveals the pleats and folds of the manipulations very well. It would be difficult to actively dislike the material due to its neutral colour and composition; consequently one can give items made from calico to anybody. There are few places where this cloth will look out of place.

The type of calico that I normally use is an inexpensive medium-weight firmly woven material which can be purchased in many places from department stores to local street markets and dressmaking, interior design and quilt shops. It comes in a variety of widths and shades of cream, often with an attractive dark fleck. You may find a slightly 'stiffer' (more dressing) material easier to manipulate, rather than the lovely sheer calico/muslin used for backing quilts and/or hand-quilting. This latter type is a trifle fine for easy manipulation and is not so easy to piece as the crisper cloth; but it really does not matter too much if you are careful. Some of the techniques will lend themselves to a thinner weight of fabric, others to a more firmly woven heavier weight of cloth. To make the designs in miniature, I would advise use of finely woven light-weight material.

## Use of Colour

Traditionally the major pattern within each block will be composed from one or more colours with the background material remaining all the same. There is no reason why you can't use a variety of colours - use up all the scraps - then keep the sashing bands to a uniform hue which will co-ordinate the creation.

Any combination of colours may be used, but it is noticeable that the lighter the hue the more the texture will show. Black or very dark shades may obscure the intended impression but I have seen some fascinating pieces created from black chintz. Black and white can be an amazing partnership (see photograph). As a beginner you may prefer to use paler tints to start with. Patterned fabric can have an interesting effect, but the pattern should not be too large or the textural definition becomes lost and the shapes tend to merge.

There are many books which offer advice on colour selection and one can become totally confused with the enormous selection of materials available. A minimum of four complementary or contrasting tints, tones and shades will be needed. This is the smallest number that can be used in any one design which ensures that no two colours have to touch each other. As soon as two identically coloured sections butt together the general appearance of the design will change, because these two will merge giving the optical illusion of a larger segment and the original design will be lost.

When selecting the range of colours think about including a stronger or darker shade to add some contrast and definition to the patterns. If all the colours are of the same tonal quality then the 'dynamics of the design' will be lost (favourite phrase - always sounds really good!). To be serious, you will not go far wrong if you select a range of colours that lie side by side on the colour wheel. These are referred to as analogous i.e. in agreement with each other. Using colours directly opposite on the wheel - complementary - can be harder as they really need to be used in the correction proportion.

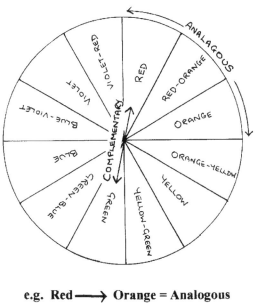

e.g. Red ⟶ Orange = Analogous
e.g. Red & Green = Complementary

For instance, if you mix purple and yellow together then nine parts of the total piece should be purple and three parts should be yellow and these proportions vary depending on which two opposing colours you select. For more information see chaps like Goethe and Itten and study their colour theories.

*This can all get very complicated and my best advice would be to seek the help of the store/shop owner and staff. They are usually only too happy to help.*

The final destination of the quilt may determine the choice of colour such as the decor of the room or the personal likes and dislikes of the recipient. If you are totally stuck for an idea why not look at an object or a painting or some fabric you like and use the colours therein and the proportions thereof as a starting place? What ever you choose - don't panic about it - just enjoy the making of the piece, after all you can always dye it a different colour at a later date. Remember that you could use just one colour and make a monochromatically textured and twiddled creation!

*Tip: If your selected design contains a number of pieces and you have difficulty in deciding where to place any colours, photocopy the block pattern and shade in the spaces with crayons or pencils in the relevant hues.*

## How Much Fabric do you Buy?

The most difficult problem. This will relate totally to the final size of the completed work. Each section gives an approximate guide to how much material is needed. As a rough ballpark figure a 6 ft (180cm) x 6 ft (180cm) double quilt requires 10/11 yards/metres approximately and a 6 ft(180cm) x 3 ft(90cm) single one about 5/6 yards/metres.

You may decide on a smaller creation or just make some bags or cushions in which case the total yardage can be guesstimated fairly easily. Should you decide to make an enormous king-sized quilt, then the only advice I can offer is to buy plenty of fabric and get it finished quickly, before the shop runs out of the fabric or it is discontinued.

Starting with a carefully calculated totally specific plan of action can be unproductive. As the work develops you can change your mind on size, shape and overall format, and then it becomes apparent that the carefully planned paper sketch of colour and layout does not relate at all. All those acres of that stunning sky-blue pink tint that you coloured in so carefully on the drawing look completely disgusting in reality, and you have just got to change it for something absolutely different. Making anything out of one fabric is much easier for calculating quantities. My advice is to just let it happen - relax and enjoy the creative experience and *buy plenty of material*. You can always use up the leftovers for presents. Aged aunts are delighted to receive gifts and they are generally too polite to say that the colour combination is a little odd!

*Each section indicates the MINIMUM total length (down selvedge) of fabric you would need to PURCHASE for that particular block. This amount is deliberately generous to allow for any trimming of the edges. Considerably less fabric would be required if you were using your own existing stash. A cutting plan for the pieces of some of the blocks is also included.*

## Washing the Fabrics

On the subject of laundering, I have to admit that I never pre-wash most of my fabrics. There are three reasons for this: first, I am too lazy to iron out the creases; have you ever tried pressing over-dried calico? Second, and more important the dressing in the cloth stiffens it. You will appreciate anything that is a little stiffer is probably easier to manipulate. Thirdly, using such a multitude of small pieces to create the patterns, the shrinking is so minimal that it does not appear to have any effect. *BUT I always wash the large piece of material that I use for backing the final masterpiece.* However I would advise laundering the material if it is to be used for babies or toddlers, and certainly test the darker colours for colour-fastness. Some of the dark reds, deep blues and bottle greens may bleed in the washing process and this can be disastrous. As a general rule if you prefer to pre-wash then do so and try spray starch to add the extra 'body'; but if you like the lazier method then don't pre-wash and take the gamble.

# Equipment

Quiltmaking needs very little equipment but there are some really useful gadgets that will speed up the process. Traditionally you sat down with a bag full of scraps, needle and thread, card to make templates, and off you went. Today's quilter has a whole host of tools at his/her command, some of which are excellent and some of which are not so good (says she carefully). A vast array of businesses have sprung up supplying a multifarious selection of contraptions and we are all apt to fall for the latest rage in natty notions. I have spent pounds on new bits and pieces to end up using the same tried and tested range of equipment.

You will need:

cutting out tools/equipment
general sewing accessories & threads
marking/drawing/measuring instruments
sewing machine

## Cutting Out Tools/Equipment

Rotary cutter, board and ruler are advisable. Don't panic if you do not possess these items - all the techniques in the book can be done the traditional way by drawing, measuring, making card templates and cutting with a pair of scissors. This is slow and not always so accurate. There are several companies manufacturing rotary cutting tools which are usually sold in craft, needlework, dressmaking and quilting establishments. Find such a shop and seek their advice and/or ask your friends for their suggestions on the choice of equipment. Prices vary enormously so shop around if you can before you buy. (Further information on Rotary equipment can be found in **'Tucks Textures & Pleats'** pages 6 - 9.)

## General Sewing Accessories

_**Small sharp scissors, paper scissors and decent cutting scissors**_ are vital to any needlewoman/man (can't stand use of word 'person'). I presume that you will have a selection of _**needles**_ and _**pins**_. The bestest pins in my opinion are the 'flower' headed ones as they are very fine, sharp and long, ideal for pinning many layers, easy to use if the hands are not so flexible, and lie flat underneath a ruler (doesn't wobble on the lumpy pinheads). _**Masking tape, thimbles**_ etc. etc.

## Choice of Threads

Ideally I would suggest pure cotton thread but this is not always readily available and is expensive. Polyester or a mixed blend would be a good substitute but do watch the thread count. Thread count or thickness depends on the width of the fibre; it becomes thinner as the count gets higher, i.e. 50 is finer than 40. Average sewing thread is 40 for normal sewing and 50 for machine embroidery.

## Marking/drawing/measuring Instruments

*Accurate ruler and tape measure* are really useful plus a *pair of compasses, protractor and set square* for any geometric drawing. In my opinion *pencils* are preferable for marking; use a sharp H rather than a soft leaded one (harder lead leaves less graphite on the cloth and is less likely to smear). Soap or chalk may also be used (these either wash or rub out easily). There are many varieties of chemical marking pens available, some of which wash out and some of which don't: be careful and test them first. Occasionally the pen marks return as you press the work, which is disastrous.

## Sewing Machine

Any basic machine is fine although a swing-needle (machine does a zigzag) would be an added advantage. *You do not need a fancy model*. I frequently get asked for advice on purchasing a new one and can whole-heartedly recommend a Bernina but both Pfaff and Husquarvna-Viking have equally admirable qualities. When I first started sewing back in 1988, I asked all the top people in every sewing field what machine they had - all seemed to possess a Bernina somewhere so I bought one. This has proved to be very good (I now have two) but if I had enough money I would have a Pfaff and Viking in addition. Sewing machines are very personal and what suits one person certainly doesn't suit another - *do your homework before you purchase anything*. The last piece of advice is to dissuade the nearest and dearest from getting one as a surprise; sadly they are apt to spend a 'squillion-squid' on the wrong one!!!

## Sewing Machine Needles

Unlike thread counts, machine needles get thicker as the numbers increase. As a general rule use thinner needles (lower number) for sewing finer fabrics and thicker needles for coarser material (higher number). The sizes are printed on the packet and are generally in both European and British sizing :-

65 = 9; 70 = 10; 75 = 1; 80 = 12; 90 = 14; 100 = 16; 120 = 18

There is a huge range to choose from but watch that you buy the correct ones. I personally prefer the 'sharp' pointed needles because I use mainly natural (non-man-made) materials and would only select 'ball-point' needles for synthetics and stretch fabrics. Sharps are very hard to find these days and have been widely replaced by a Universal needle; these are supposedly suitable for all fibres including stretch materials, but you may find that they are not the best for silks or tightly woven fabrics such as chintz. Instruction manuals do not wax lyrical on the correct size and type of needle to use, but it does make a tremendous difference to the finished effect.

The other major piece of advice is to change the needle fairly frequently and throw it away - do not re-use blunt needles. Blunt or damaged needles may cause skipped stitches and damage to the fibres. Also *dispose of any needles safely*; I take mine every so often to the pharmacist/chemist and ask him to dispose of them. *Last little word of wisdom: when you change your needle make sure that it is properly inserted and pushed up into the slot - many sewing machine faults are caused by poor needle insertion.*

# Important Information

### Seam Allowances and Measurements for Sampler Quilts

*All the blocks are designed to measure 12"(30cm) square when completely finished. Most of the time the seam allowance is ¼"(0.5cm) but there are times when this changes so BE CAREFUL and READ THE INSTRUCTIONS.*

The shapes must be cut out at the correct size and you must select *either* inches (*imperial*) or centimetres (*metric*) for each and every item. *Each shape must be cut exactly to size so think before you cut.*

Every block should measure *12½"(31cm)* on completing the internal piecing of the block (still has raw outer edges) and *12"(30cm)* when bordered (framed) ready for stitching together in the final assembly. Confusion is easy with so many different measurements bandied about. For the purposes of all calculations the rule is:

> *Always work on the desired finished size and then add on seam allowances .*

Consequently to achieve a 'finished' *6"(15cm) square* one must *cut 6½"(16cm)* piece to start.

### Working in Inches (Imperial)

It is most important to sew an accurate ¼" seam. Stitch a sample and check the seam - don't just guess it. Sometimes we assume that we know exactly how to stitch a ¼" but it is well worth double-checking. Many machine manufacturers provide a ¼" foot (No. 37 for Bernina owners) and this is readily available from your stockist. Alternatively, try moving the needle either nearer to or further from the inner edge of the presser foot or some part of the foot that you can use as a guide; make a note of the setting and check it. *Read the instruction book*. (I would love £5 for every time that I have shown a student how to move their needle setting). Some machines have sole-plates with the measurements inscribed and the more mature machines are often fitted with imperial measured presser feet.

If your machine has a dial or knob which can move the needle by turning or sliding in some way it is usually possible to position the knob midway between two points, thus setting the needle ¼" from the inner edge of the presser foot. (Older Elnas, Frister Rossmanns, many Singers and a few other makes operate this way.)

The up-to-date 'techo-computerised' machines have a wide choice of needle settings so experiment before you rush out and purchase a new foot. Almost certainly the latest Bernina 180, Pfaffs and Husquarvna-Vikings can be aligned to ¼" by adjusting the needle position.

### Metric Measurements

Technically ¼" does not translate as 0.5cm exactly. The reason for selecting 0.5cm and not an exact translation is purely for simplifying the mathematics. Each of the individual shapes must be cut out with the seam allowances included, and it is much easier to cut out at 0.5cm intervals rather than some curious measurement which will not align easily with the metric cutting tools. _**Not all the given measurements are translated into the exact metric equivalent**_ for simplicity of both cutting and mathematical calculations.

## Sewing Terms

There are certain words that alter in context from country to country. To save confusion here are some of them:

**Tacking** (Britain) = **Basting** (USA) - long stitches designed to secure layers.
**Catching** (Britain) = **Tacking** (USA) - small stitch to secure firmly in place.
**Cross-grain** (USA) = cut from selvedge to selvedge.
**Calico** (Britain) = **Muslin** (USA). A loom state (as natural) cotton cloth.
**Calico** (USA) = Printed cotton fabric often floral in design (Britain)
**Muslin** (Britain) = **Cheesecloth** (USA)
**Vilene** (Britain) = **Stabilizer** (USA)

There are others but use your common sense - everything will be fine unless you tell American gentlemen that you are quite capable of 'humping your own bags' and don't tell the ladies to 'sew faster and whizz along those seams'!!

## Cutting Fabric

Please please _**do not rip**_ the pieces out. Ripping causes distortion of the fibres, increases the fraying factor and stretches and damages the edge. Torn out squares are not as accurate as cut ones. Today's modern mechanical weaving processes are not as accurate as they might be, and tearing across the weft (side to side) grain can produce a diagonal tear. Only rip if you need a frayed edge.

In my opinion any strips of fabric should always be cut across the material on the weft grain - from selvedge to selvedge. Cutting in this fashion ensures that you have a little more 'give' in the fibres and the pieces will lie more happily.

Ideally all the grains of all the pieces should flow in harmony - the warp threads lying top to bottom and the weft running side to side. Technically a totally perfect piece of patching would have the grains lying exactly as they did when woven originally. It would be extremely expensive to cut every piece so that the final arrangement had the grain going this way. the weft grain is more

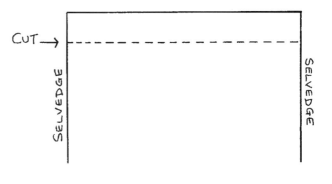

flexible than the warp (which is taut) and it doesn't matter quite so much if it runs top to bottom instead of side to side. Try to keep either horizontal or vertical if at all possible.

I have seen many quilts with wavy edges hanging at exhibitions. Quite frequently this is caused by the maker desiring to have the border in one continuous strip: he/she has purchased the required length of material, cut the strips and attached them. As these strips are cut down the warp they are much tighter and can drag the other sections thus causing a certain degree of buckling. The only time when you have to do this is when working with a specific directional design. Should buckling occur heavy quilting will disguise it.

For some reason patchworkers cut their pieces out willy-nilly in every direction then wonder why the work stretches in strange fashions. Dressmakers are very aware of the grain lines and cut the patterns accordingly. Soft furnishers do not hang curtains sideways so it seems logical to apply the same rules to any piecing.

Finally, I would seriously suggest that you never stitch a bias grain to a straight grain - they fight and buckle. Stitch bias to bias, they flow together, and stitch straight to straight, preferably weft to weft.

## Pressing Seams

To reduce bulk press all seams open and flat. This is not as strong as pushing the seams to one side but it makes the work have a flatter appearance and is easier to quilt. Seams pushed to the same side form a ridge which may be unsightly. Opening the seams can aid successful piecing as the junctions of the joined shapes can be seen more easily.

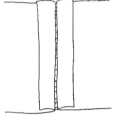

Whether you use steam or not depends on the fabric but should you inadvertently singe the material a _weak_ solution of hydrogen peroxide (available from chemist/pharmacists) will remove most of the mark. Apply with a dry cloth and dab over the stain.

## Diagrams/Figures

_These are not always drawn to scale; sometimes the important feature is exaggerated to emphasise the point being made._

_Figures and diagrams are NOT numbered if the related text is immediately adjacent. Numbers are only given if the drawing is not beside the relevant text._

**Luscious Lily Block**
with appliquéd leaves (page 29)

# Dutchman's Puzzle

Although this has nothing whatsoever to do with a Dutchman, one of my small adventures into the world of man-hunting did cause a degree of bewilderment for one gentleman. As you will be aware from the foreword I tried my hand at replying to adverts in the 'The Times' and had a set letter previously composed on the computer that I would specifically alter for each individual advert (filed under 'Seek Gent'). The letter had to answer the advertisement and give a short resume of me as a person. I described myself as:

*5' 5", 41 years old, divorced, slim (8st 4lbs depending on which side of the scales I lean) medium build, short fair-red unruly-curly hair, wear glasses, have totally unnoticeable wooden leg! two glass eyes and a cauliflower ear. Possess an eccentric 'Heinz '57 variety dog and a son aged 20 at university etc etc. (Time has passed on and I am not so young but possibly slightly scraggier and no longer have the dog. The son exists nethertheless, no wiser, a trifle older and still at university! Do they ever leave home?)*

The gentleman concerned had written in his advert that he wanted a lady who would look good and be at ease in a Barbour, a Balmain or a bikini. The reply he got, in addition to the above blurb, was that I possessed an anorak, a Gucci and a two-piece. He was entranced or to be more honest, interested enough to ring me. We had the usual exchange of niceties then he proposed a meeting but expressed great concern at my wooden leg seemingly to be very bothered by it; did it give me any trouble? - did it show very much? - could I drive with it? Naturally, I reassured him on all these matters. We agreed the time. Naughtily, I borrowed a crutch from a friend plus a white stick (remember the glass eye), arrived at the allotted place, got out of the car to find no prospective 'cher-ami'. As I waited leaning on the crutch, tapping the stick, I saw a car detach itself from a partially concealed space in the car park and drive off. He never turned up and I shall always wonder whether he saw the accoutrements and decided he just couldn't cope, so slunk off. Moral of the story - don't try to be a real smarty-pants as jokes can backfire and maybe I missed out on a really wonderful catch. Still, he didn't have a sense of humour or maybe he believed the tale of the wood-worm in my prosthesis!

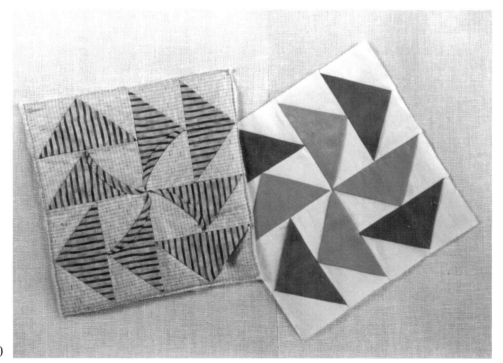

'Calico Creation' (72" x 72") featuring block designs from all three books. Centre panel constructed from Trumpets, Corners on Log Cabin and a Star Flower. Outer edge (reading from top left clockwise) Tucked Up Fan, Dutchmans Puzzle, Eight Petal Flower, Multiple Origami Twist, Tucked Up Fan, Textured Star, Driven Dotty, Interlocked Triangles, Luscious Lilies, Origami Twist, Trumpet Voluntary, another Origami Twist, Luscious Lilies, Hexagonal Origami Twist, Triangle Cornet, Interlocked Hexagons, machine pieced & quilted. (Jennie Rayment).

Lap quilt (45" x 45") - constructed from Corners on Log Cabin, Stuffed Squares, Multiple Origami Twist, Dutchmans Puzzle, Trumpets & Interlocked Squares, machine pieced & quilted. (Joan Sortwell)

'It's in the Book' (65" x 77") - created mainly from designs featured in 'Tucked Up in Bed'. (Shelagh Jarvis).

Stripy samples show Four Pointed Flower, Dutchmans Puzzle and Stuffed Squares. (Jennie Rayment).

Multicoloured Doofah cushion (15" square) with a miniature one in the centre. (Jennie Rayment).

## Dutchman's Puzzle

The Dutchman's Puzzle is the name of traditional American patchwork design. The original concept required triangular templates but this one is constructed from rectangles and squares only. It is very simple to piece yet has room for a little manipulative twiddling and fiddling if desired. Explore the effect of different colours, and why not use up some scraps?

Minimum yards/metres for total block in one colour: 11"(28cm) x 44"(115cm)

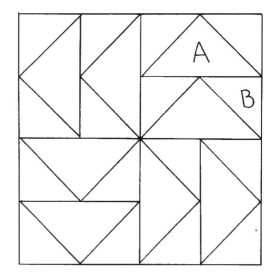

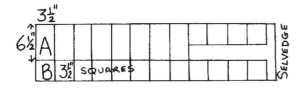

### Preparing the Pieces

1. Use the rotary cutter and ruler to cut the following squares and rectangles. If you do not possess this equipment then make card templates; draw round and cut out. Remember to trim selvedges.

*To make the larger (A) triangles cut:*

Eight rectangles - 3½"(8.5cm) x 6½"(16cm)
Using two colours - cut four of each or any other combination of your choice.

*For B sections from the background material cut:*

Sixteen 3½"(8.5cm) squares
(Change the design by replacing some of the background fabric squares with additional colours if preferred.)

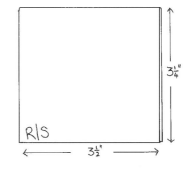

2. With R/S on outside, fold all the rectangles in half length-ways forming a 3¼"(8cm) x 3½"(8.5cm) shape; press lightly.

### Start Stitching - *Seam allowances ¼"(0.5cm)*

1. Place one folded rectangle on to one square ensuring that the folded edge is ¼"(0.5cm) from top of square, aligning all raw edges; *pin well as in the diagram on next page.* (If there is any chance that the layers may slip, baste (using a long stitch length) the folded rectangle to the square - keep basting just within the ¼"(0.5cm) seam allowance.) Repeat seven more times. *Work systematically - each piece should be identical.*

2. Lay the remaining squares on top of the pinned/basted shapes - 'sandwiching' the shape; stitch the seam. Do stitch the pinned side i.e. down the folded side of the rectangle. Sew towards the four raw corners. The folded rectangle is now inserted in the seam of the two squares. Press *all* the back seams open (remove any basting). On opening the back seam you will see a small rounded fold, like a little 'nose' in the top of the folded and inserted rectangle seam - squash this flat.

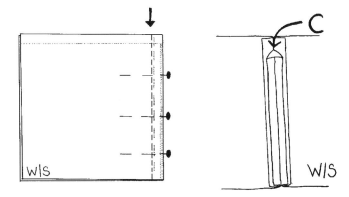

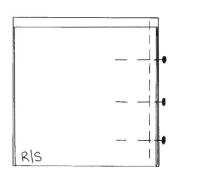

3. Open the rectangle by pulling the two corners apart; flatten gently and amazingly there is a triangle! Arrange as in drawing. Press in place. The shape can be stuffed at this stage - insert a small quantity of torn wadding/batting; push up into the shape; do not over-stuff. Pin this opening to the stitched squares ensuring that *all raw edges are matching*. Now baste the open edge of the shape to the squares as in the diagram through all layers. Keep the basting within ¼"(0.5cm) S/A.

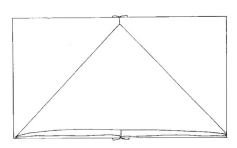

4. Repeat seven more times with the remaining pieces. Lay out all the pieces to form the design as shown below.

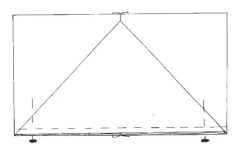

5. Sew together in pairs to form squares. Select two sections, lay R/Ss together as in Fig. 1 - *double-check that you stitch the correct seam*. Pin if desired. Aim to sew exactly through the point of that odd little 'nose' at **C** which you so carefully pressed - the base of this shape is the top of the inserted rectangle. After stitching; press the seam open. Repeat with the other three sets to form four squares.

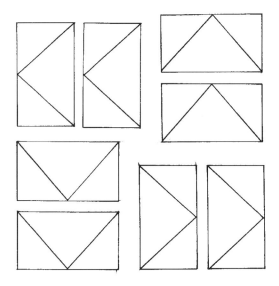

Fig. 1

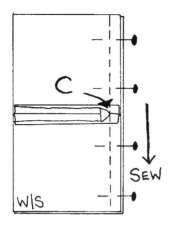

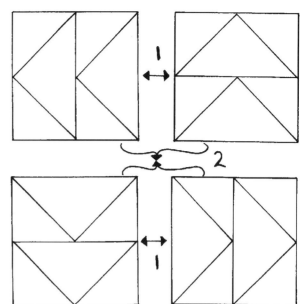

6. Sew all the squares together. Sew two to form a rectangle (stage 1); repeat with the remaining two. Sew the two rectangles (stage 2) to form the final block, and press all the seams open to reduce bulkiness. If desired remove any basting. When stitching together try to line up all the seams and points and sew through the very tip of any points.

By examining the open pressed seam one can see a division - where the division emerges from the seam is the top of the inserted shape. Try to stitch exactly through this mark as in the diagram.

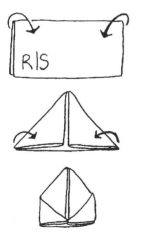

7. The edges of the shapes can be rolled back in a variety of ways: roll the entire edge or only a part, or catch it in the centre and roll both sides. What about tucking an insertion into the pocket such as a Somerset (folded/mitred) type square (Sharkstooth USA)? Alternatively, try a Baltimore Rosebud which is a Somerset square refolded as in left-hand diagram below to resemble a petal. Use the blind hem stitch to secure the rollback or do it by hand with a tiny hem, running or even a stab stitch.

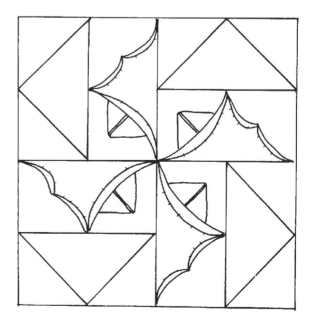

# Luscious Lilies

The 'Lily' block has long been a favourite with Patchwork aficionados and had always required a modicum of skill in both the cutting of all the shapes and in piecing them together. This wholly new method of construction is free from any specially shaped templates as you will only require a series of squares. In addition, there are all kinds of possibilities for a little manipulation of the pieces!

Perhaps I should quote Solomon who, in all his glory was not arrayed like one of these etc., and I hazard a guess that he would not be able to construct this particular piece so easily. Back in them there days, there were no interesting gadgets like rotary cutters, mats, rulers and surprisingly enough there were no sewing machines. The first machine was invented by the Singer Company in America back in the 1800's and has recently developed at a great rate of knots into 'all-singing-and-dancing' machines which are really computers that sew. One day they will even be able to make a cup of tea, as it is you can go off and leave the machine to embroider a design while you snooze or better still go down the pub!

As a tutor it is very important that I can understand the fundamental rudiments of all machines, but at times even I am completely foxed. There are occasions when one is totally dumbfounded by the way people treat their machines. These poor little inoffensive and inanimate objects *do like* being cleaned out and oiled in various places (where stated in the instruction manual). They have moving parts and moving parts like a little lubrication - don't we all!! So fellow readers take a moment to clean that dear little object and add just a touch of sewing machine oil (*never ever* use anything else especially not cooking oil).

To digress for a moment - Solomon reminds me of the time when I used to swim on a regular basis in a futile attempt to keep fit. My biggest problem whilst plodding up and down the swimming pool is my inability to see. I am very short-sighted and am unable to wear glasses while swimming; this makes the other swimmers a trifle blurred! I usually wear glasses to the pool side, remove and swim myopically. One morning, I spotted this exceedingly trim and attractive looking guy who sported a rather snazzy pair of really distinctive trunks and very flash goggles. He took no notice of me despite the smiles I gave him whenever we passed. Time passed and I kept seeing him in the pool. Wow! He really seemed a bit of all right! I imagined various different scenarios in my mind - interesting romantic situations where he would carry me off into the dim blue yonder etc. It passed through my mind that I could pretend to be drowning; he would cleave his way through the storm tossed, white-crested billowing waves (in the swimming pool?), rescue me and give mouth to mouth resuscitation whilst gazing lovingly into my eyes. Sorrowfully, I recollected the lifeguard sitting by the poolside. Knowing my luck, he'd rescue me and a more pimply, bedraggled and unprepossessing youth would be difficult to find. All these wild imaginings passed the time amazingly and I swam lots of lengths. Then one morning, I met him by the pool just before I removed my glasses. He must have been **ninety** if a day, bald as a coot and the trim physique was in need of a good iron. Talk about a wrinkly!! Perhaps I should think about the lifeguard instead; was I that desperate?

## Luscious Lily Block (photo on page 19)

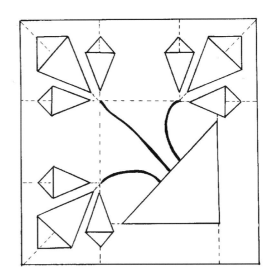

You may to choose to make the design as a small hanging (see colour photographs opposite page 79), but why not try just one panel and make a cushion or use it for the side of a bag, a quilt block, a table mat etc. etc? Go wild and make dozens of panels for a cot/single/double bed quilt, lap quilt or a tablecloth. This is a really user-friendly patchwork which is equally easy by hand or machine. Machining is the fastest option and you don't need to be terribly skilled!

Minimum quantity of fabric for total block in one colour: 12"(30cm) x 44"(115cm)

As the flowers are all made from squares, why not use up all those cotton scraps and have multicoloured flower petals? Plan the colours by shading in a copy of the diagram. Hopefully, you will then get the selected colours in the chosen places.

### Preparing the Pieces

1. Use the rotary cutter and ruler to cut the following squares and strips. Remove selvedge first. If you do not possess rotary cutting equipment (like Solomon) then draw the various square sizes on to a piece of graph paper; cut out carefully and glue to thin card; use these as templates. Place the templates on the W/S of cloth and draw carefully round; preferably use a *hard sharp pencil* - watch that you cut inside the pencil mark as the drawn line is outside the template and that little extra amount fractionally changes the size of the cut square. Make the strips by cutting a 2½"(6.5cm) strip across the full width of the material then chopping into the relevant sized chunks.

*To make the flower shapes and the pot cut:*
Large Flowers - Three 4½"(11.5cm) squares: Small Flowers - Six 3"(7.5cm)
Flower Pot - One 5½"(14cm) square.

*From the background material cut :*
Three 4 ⁷/₈"(12.25cm) squares: Two 4½"(11cm) squares: One 6½"(16.5cm) square:
One {2½"(6.5cm) x 6½"(16.5cm)} strip: One {2½"(6.5cm) x 8½"(22cm)} strip.

*For stems:* Scrap 9"(23cm) or so square required if using bias binding technique
(Stems can be made in a variety of different methods - see page 28)

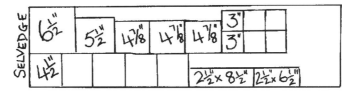

25

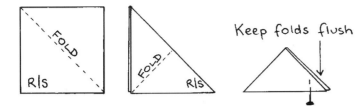

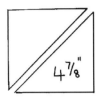

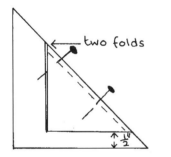

2. Gently finger press all the Flower and Pot squares in half on the diagonal forming a triangle; R/S outside.

Fold Flower shapes *again* to make a smaller triangle; pin the layers together; *ensure that the two folds are flush.*

3. Cut the three 4⅞"(12.25cm) squares of background material in half diagonally, forming six triangles.

## Start Stitching

### ALL SEAM ALLOWANCES ARE ¼"(0.5cm) AND MUST BE ACCURATE!

1. Use *longest* stitch on machine to baste the raw edges of the Flower triangles; keep the stitching within the ¼"(0.5cm) seam. Start at the two folds and sew towards the other end. I tried cheating and avoiding this but all the raw edges slide and the folds don't line up.

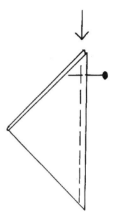

2. Take *two of the triangles* (i.e. one 4⅞" (12.25cm) square divided in two); place one large Flower on one triangular shape lining up the raw edge of Flower with the raw diagonal edge of triangle; *position ½"(1cm) up from raw edge* - check that the open end (two folds) is furthest away from this end - *look at the diagram carefully*.

Pin; lay the second triangle on top (R/S together) and sew the diagonal edge (use ¼"(0.5cm seam), try not to stretch the bias edge. The Flower is now trapped in the seam and the resulting square should measure 4½"(11.5cm). Press the seam open; fussy bods can unpick the basting and open out the seam of the Flower (bet you wished you had remembered to baste with a long stitch!). Repeat with all large Flowers forming three squares in total.

3. Select one small Flower and position on the square exactly as shown in diagram keeping the open end (two folds) away from the corner of the square (**A**) (facing the same way as the larger Flower); raw edges of Flower to raw side of square with single folded side ¼"(0.5cm) from the central diagonal seam: baste. (Folded edge of Flower aligns with raw edge of underside seam.)

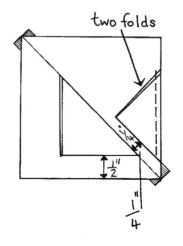

Add next Flower on the other side at the same distance; baste. Repeat on all other squares; do not be tempted to open the shapes out at this stage, leave them flat - we will play later. Trim the little 'ears' off all three squares.

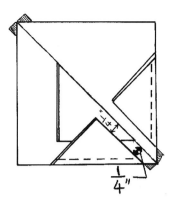

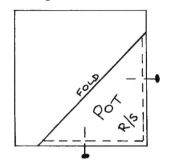

4. Fold the Flower Pot in half diagonally R/S out; press. Place on the 6½"(16.5cm) square (R/S up) aligning the corners; pin and baste - don't cheat!

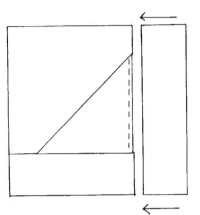

Attach the 2½"(6.5cm) x 6½"(16.5cm) strip to one side of Pot. Add the 2½"(6.5cm) x 8½"(22cm) down the other side.

5. Collect the 3 Flower segments, two 4½"(11.5cm) squares and the enlarged Pot section. Lay out to form design - *check that all the sections are the correct way round*. Stitch together to form the block as in drawing; with luck they will all fit but there's nothing like a bit of a pull and push. Join **A** to **B**; attach to Pot square: join **C,D,E**; stitch in place.

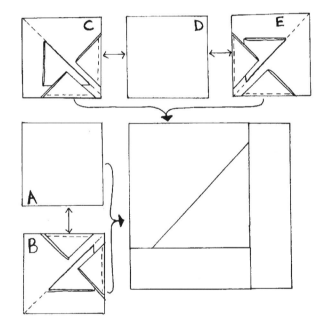

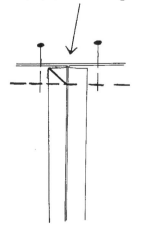

Press all the seams open where possible. Look closely at the opened seam and find the small '\/' shape (created by the junctions of the seams) - have courage to sew right through the base of the '\/' when you piece the sections. This will help to keep the 'points' accurate. (Sometimes you will have to press the thick seams of the inserts (Flower shapes) to one side unless all the basting is removed. Don't worry the extra 'wadge' will be absorbed by the wadding/batting when you finally quilt the work.)

6. Using a pencil, lightly draw in the stems. How about embroidering the stems by hand or use a solid satin stitch on the machine? Why not create the stalks from an applied bias strip? Tuck the ends of the bands at least 1"(2.5cm) into the Pot. This will prevent them coming loose should you choose to roll the edge of the Pot back for further textural enhancement. The other end can be inserted into a small hole in seam under the flower; re-stitch afterwards.

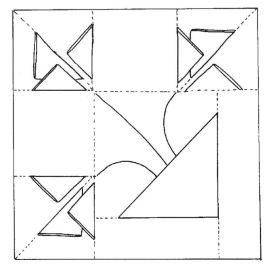

## Making Bias Strips

Construct bands with a bias binding maker or purchase ready-prepared bias binding, but these may be too wide for the design. You could refold the strips in half - this is very bulky or you could trim one edge and repress the fold). Sometimes the width of the strips varies when they are only folded and pressed but not stitched in any way. Strips could also be prepared with Bias Bars, but this method produces a seam on the back which may be lumpy unless you trim and press very carefully. The method described below has two advantages - the strip is totally flat on the underside and all the edges are held firm with the basting.

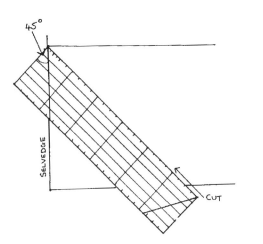

Place the 45° line on the ruler down the selvedge; cut up the side of the ruler - this makes a bias edge (diagonal cut); cut three 1¼"(3cm) strips from this edge. The strips will not have to be joined but should you ever need to do so, join by placing at right-angles with R/Ss together aligning raw edges;

## Rayment's Bias Strip Technique

1. Cut the bias strips from the 9"(23cm) square. The best way to prepare the bias strips is to use the rotary cutter, ruler and cutting mat. (There is a method of making a continuous bias strip by cutting a square; dividing the square on the diagonal; re-stitching back together and drawing lines then forming a cylinder etc. There are several drawbacks to this method and it is not one that I would recommend, but use it if you like.

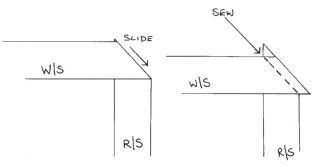

slide top strip up (keeping diagonal edges together); stitch through the junction: trim and press seams open. *Sew exactly down the point where the two fabrics cross for really straight seam joins.*

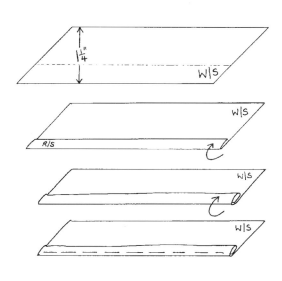

2. Lay bias strip W/S up on the ironing board; press ¼"(0.5cm) fold along one side (draw a line ½"(1cm) from raw edge if necessary - press to the line). Fold over again keeping the measurement at ¼"(0.5cm) and press again (just like making a small hem). Check that the second fold is parallel to the raw edge. Tack either by hand or use a really *long* stitch length on the sewing machine; use a contrasting coloured thread keeping any knotted ends on the top side. *KEEP tacking to the outer folded side.*

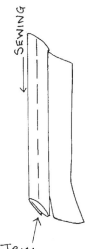

3. Turn band over and trim excess material back to the tacking line. Use small sharp scissors held at an angle so you do not cut the strip. Cutting up the strip towards the start of the basting stitching is easiest. Ensure no raw edges show on the right side. This is called the 'Rayment' method and was invented by myself - I'll tell you the story another day!

4. Starting from the Pot remembering to tuck the raw ends in by at least 1"(2.5cm). Tack the strips by hand over the drawn or stitched lines; centring the line under the strip. Manipulate the bias band firmly round the curved section. It is advisable to tack with contrasting thread (easier to see when unpicking) and with diagonal stitches to hold the strips more firmly.

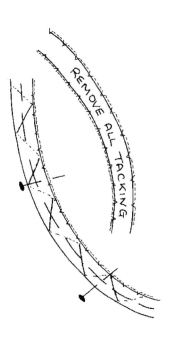

5. Using a very small slip or hem stitch sew both sides of the strip. Catching the edge of the fabric with a straight stitch rather than a diagonal one makes it less visible; use toning/matching thread with small firm stitches - do not pull the thread too tight as this buckles the work. Try machine stitching round the strips. The blind hem stitch is very useful for this method - setting the stitch length at **1** and stitch width at **1** (these measurements apply to most machines although some of the really new ones particularly Husquarvana-Viking computerised models may need a different stitch setting). Ideally the small **straight stitches run outside** the strip and the **indentation catches the edge of the bias band**. Be aware that not all machines will adjust both the stitch settings, sometimes the stitch width is pre-set and it is not possible to change it. Use of an open fronted presser foot will help - then you can see where you are going!

If preferred, sew round the design with a small straight stitch, a fine zigzag or any other pattern to enhance the effect.

6. Pull out both sets of the tacking stitches on completion of the sewing. Press gently and admire.

*(This method can be use for all designs that require a Bias Strip such as 'Stained Glass Window' or 'Celtic Appliqué'.)*

### Completing the Creation

Now you can play with the flower shapes - they can be opened out and squashed; pulled downwards and caught in relevant places, stuffed, rolled and/or manipulated in any way/shape or fashion that you choose. You could even just leave them untwiddled but it is a little boring - use your imagination and pull them around a bit. Try tucking in some small folded squares. Once you have decided on the shape then secure it at the relevant point with a small stitch through to background material.

Why not add some leaves to the design as shown in the photo on page 19?

The edge of the pot will roll back and can be slipped-stitched or machined down - again through all the layers. How about inserting a little torn wadding to give the pot a raised appearance before stitching down? Blind hem stitch is very useful for securing the rolled edge (see stage 5) but you may have to put the walking foot onto the machine or uneven dragging of one of the layers may occur. If in doubt do it by hand. Sacrilege, I know to all you ardent machine boffins, but why run the risk of this happening when five minutes by hand does the job nicely!!

The basis for this idea came from developing the ''Trumpet' idea as featured in **'Tucks Textures & Pleats'**. See if you can apply this technique to other traditional Patchwork blocks for a really creative and fascinating effect.

Just keep playing!

# Stuffed Squares

One of my better titles for a 'Nipped and Tucked' sampler square! There are times when I am particularly blest with imagination and the day I thought of this idea was obviously one!

I shall digress as this specific title reminds me of some exceedingly Stuffed Squares that I met on my voyages through the morass of gentleman hunting. One in particular was so pedantic it just wasn't true. He insisted on coming to the meeting with a red rose in his lapel, rolled-up newspaper under his arm and said that he would be wearing a light-grey overcoat. Sadly the day proved to very warm and he was the only gentleman wearing any form of coat for miles (was getting a little pink round the gills). We duly met and he was very pleasant apart from a strong tendency to correct me on any lapses in grammar. (You will have encountered many of those already.) He expressed a wish to partake of a light repast (Goodee - a decent meal!). Guess where we went - Pizza Hut!!! Now he didn't drink (sad), didn't smoke (good), didn't seem to have any interests (boring) and said he wasn't very hungry (bother!). We would share a Pizza and he felt that water was a very beneficial liquor. There is only so long that you can push a half-pizza round a plate so the meeting was quite brief. Just as well because his main interest was 'Twitching' (bird watching), naturally I am really well acquainted with the Lesser Spotted Pink Throated Tree Borer! It was not the type of conversation where you could make 'Smart-Alec' remarks about Blue Tits!! He asked for the bill and suggested that we should share the £3.50 or so that it cost - this caused me to raise my eyebrows somewhat. Now I'm not the sort of girl who needs to be wined and dined and I'm more than happy to pay half, but when I had journeyed to see him, wasted a new hairdo, bought new tights and slathered on masses of my favourite pong, I did expect a reasonable nosh! Needless to say we did not meet again as I was not quite his type of female. He probably felt that I was an overbearing, ill-educated and demanding hussy.

There was a further Stuffed Square who was very charming and I could have coped with his stuffiness, but he brought all his latest holiday snaps to our first meeting - try keeping awake after the first hundred. He had a small boat and a caravan parked in the New Forest but despite being vaguely interesting, he was about six inches shorter than I and all he seemed to want was a person to act as ballast in the boat or it could have been the caravan, I was never really sure. I knew that I wouldn't be very good as ballast as I wriggle too much so we bid 'fare-thee-well'. I did notice that he had a slightly strange hang-up (obsession not net curtains) about postcodes (zipcodes). He waxed lyrical on the subject of addressing letters, informing me quite categorically that the post reached its destination considerably quicker if the two parts of the postcode were clearly separated. To be fair to him, he did laugh when I addressed a note to him with the postcode written -

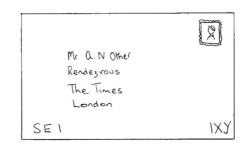

## Stuffed Squares

This is developed from the 'Interlocked Square' design described in **'Tucks & Textures Two'** and like so many of the other things, it has a multitude of twiddlable possibilities. As the design is created from lots of separate pieces you could use up scraps and there are lots possibilities for inspirational use of colour. Two versions to this pattern are described - the second has a greater potential for colour selection and manipulative manoeuvering.

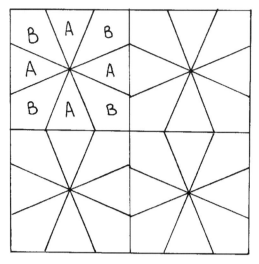

**Stuffed Squares Mark 1**

Each block is constructed from four identical units. Decide where you would like all the colours to go before you cut out the seemingly endless 3½"(8.5cm) squares.

## Stuffed Squares Mark 1

Minimum quantity of fabric for total block in 1 colour: 11"(27cm) x 44"(115cm)

### Prepare the Pieces

1. Use the rotary cutter and ruler to cut the following squares. If you do not possess this equipment then make a card template; draw round on W/S and cut out.

*To make the Stuffed Squares Mark 1 cut:*

Sixteen 3½"(8.5cm) squares for Stuffed (textured) sections - **A**

Sixteen 3½"(8.5cm) squares from the background material - **B**

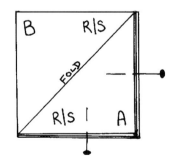

Fold all sixteen **A** squares (stuffed portions) diagonally in half, R/S on outside forming a triangle; press lightly to retain shape. Carefully position the triangles on to each of the remaining **B** squares (R/S up), aligning all raw edges and ensuring that they are all positioned to the same side of the square as in the diagram; pin in place.

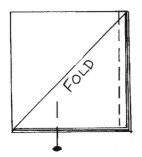

## Start Stitching - *All seam allowances ¼"(0.5cm)*

1. Baste all layers together down *one side* only - *be systematic - baste the same side of each one* (set longest machine stitch and keep inside the ¼"(0.5cm) S/A). Leave pin in the unattached corner. Divide into four sets of four basted squares and arrange each group in a pinwheel design.

2. Take one of these groups and stitch together (Fig. 1) by sewing into pairs first (step 1); matching points and folds (as in patchwork). Remove the basting (bet you wished that you had used a long stitch!) and press open both the centre seam and the seam of the textural insert - flatten the 'nose'. Now sew the two halves together (step 2) aligning all the sections in the centre. Try the pin trick - push a pin through the junctions of both sets and line up all points - put an extra pin either side of the junction and remove the centre one (Fig. 2). Alternatively, leave the first pin in place (holding the junction); sew towards junction; stop stitching just before; remove pin; aim for the hole (having noted the spot) then sew through; continue to the end of the seam. (Personally, I tend to line up the points before I stitch; peep between the layers just before reaching the vital junction and give it a little pull or a tiny push and hopefully make it fit.) Press open the centre seam and flatten 'noses'. Repeat with the remaining twelve squares forming four larger blocks in total.

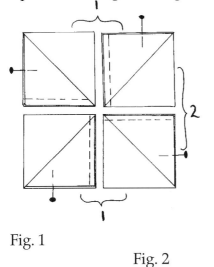

3. Select one of these larger squares; lift up the textural sections, open out and flatten; the squashed shape will protrude over the edges. Jiggle the pieces until all four match. Press in place. Square up by trimming the excess fabric. Follow the stages illustrated on the bottom.

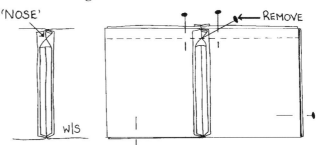

Fig. 1

Fig. 2

Hey - look - you have made little pockets! You could stuff 'em with some tiny portions of wadding/batting or whatever. Lightly stuff the pockets; pin the open end to retain stuffing as in diagram; push it down well and pin ½"(1cm) in from the outer edge. Repeat with the other three pieces. (See next page for more ideas.)

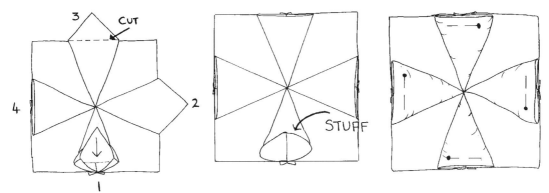

4. Stitch all four squares together as in stage 2 i.e. into pairs, then sew the rectangles to form the final square. Try to match up the padded parts (as they are only pinned one can always manipulate the shapes and make them align). Press all seams open. Remove pins and baste round outer edges to keep stuffing in place. Buttons are brilliant for concealing any misdemeanours in the piecing!

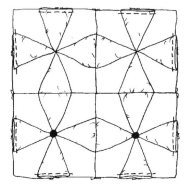

## Further Possibilities

How about omitting the stuffing, and folding the pocket shape? It can be manipulated in a number of ways.

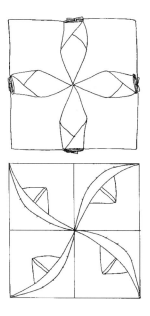

Leave the shapes to the side - don't bother about opening out; simply roll the edges and/or tuck a folded square in before rolling the edge. *Tip: stitch all four blocks together before doing textural twiddling - prevents the folds being caught in the seams.*

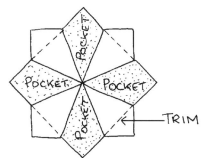

Why not trim the other corners (background fabric) not the pockets? For a slightly different appearance turn two diagonally opposite blocks through 45° and stitch together as in the illustration.

Photograph of
**Stuffed Squares Mark 2**

# Stuffed Squares Mark 2

Minimum quantity of fabric for total
block in 1 colour:
18"(45cm) x 44"(115cm)

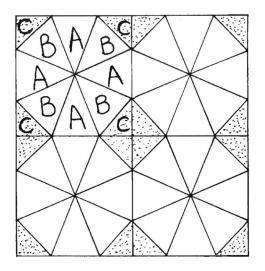

## Prepare the Pieces

1. Use the rotary cutter and ruler to cut
the following squares, or make card
templates; draw round on W/S and cut
out. Decide on position of the colours.

*For Stuffed Squares Mark 2 cut:*

Sixteen 3½″(8.5cm) squares for
Stuffed (textured) sections - **A**
Sixteen 3½″(8.5cm) squares - **B**

Four 6½″(16cm) squares from the
background material - **C**

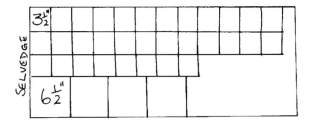

2. Fold, press and pin all **A** squares on to all **B** squares (as described on page 32).

## Start Stitching

1. Follow stages 1 - 3 in the previous section making
up the four units (stuffing if desired). *__DO NOT trim
the corners yet__*.

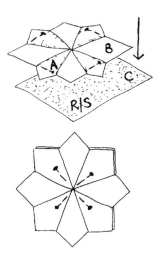

2. Lay a textured stuffed block on to one 6½″(16cm)
square  - W/S of textured block to R/S of square. Pin
layers together at the centre. Fold the  four corners
of the top section to the back i.e. tuck them under -
check that they are all folded at the same distance.
This produces more little pockets which could also
be stuffed! Fold corners under ¼″(0.5cm) in from the
edge as shown in drawing to allow for seams.

Baste round the
entire outside
edge to secure
the layers (use a
long    stitch).
Retain the pins
holding    the
stuffing in the
pockets for the
moment.

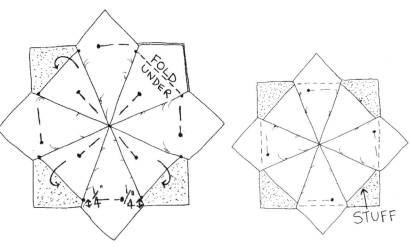

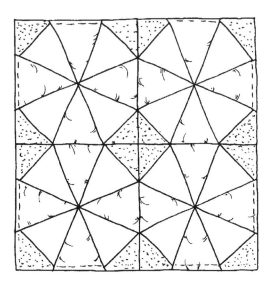

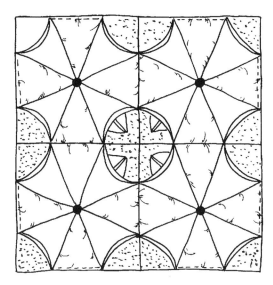

3. Repeat with the other three squares. Trim off the corners and square up. Lay the design out and sew together as in stage 2 (Stuffed Squares Mark 1). Stitch into pairs etc. (lining up all seams and padded pockets) to form the entire square. Press all seams open. Remove pins; ease the stuffing into the full shape.

**Further Possibilities**

Roll the folded edge back to give a pleasing curve. Tuck a little Somerset Patch (Sharktooth - USA) or Prairie Point into the pocket.

Add buttons for extra decoration (definitely *not* for concealing mispieced seams!)

Tuck the corner in more than suggested and/or stuff this new pocket.

Change the appearance of the design by rotating the sections as on page 34.

Add even more colour by making the 6½"(16cm) square out of four pieces (sew four 3½"(8.5cm) squares together). Fold back the corners of the top section to reveal the various tints, tones and shades of the base square.

*Now for something completely different!*

**A Dynamic 3D Doofah!**

Goodness knows what you would call this? It is an extension of the 'Interlocked Squares' technique depicted in **'Tucks & Textures Two'**. The 'doofah' may be made any size from a Christmas decoration to a giant floor cushion. It makes a really neat pincushion.

You need four squares of fabric - same size. Make a small one to begin with using four 6½"(16.5cm) squares.

1. Fold squares on the diagonal, R/S out, and press forming triangles. Lay the triangles down in the following manner, rotating each successive triangle through 90° and *tucking the last triangle under the first*. Ensure that the folded squares all touch in the centre - this is more important than the outer edges being aligned. Pin the layers carefully together as shown in the diagram.

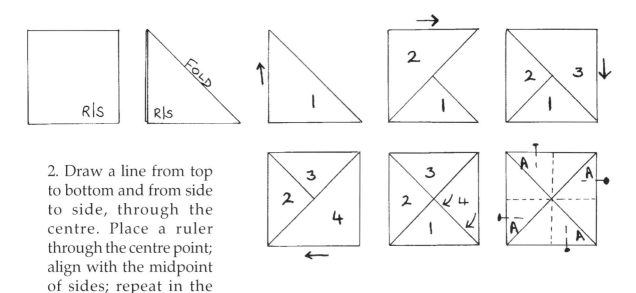

2. Draw a line from top to bottom and from side to side, through the centre. Place a ruler through the centre point; align with the midpoint of sides; repeat in the opposite direction.

3. Sew the drawn lines. Start stitching on the edge and lock the stitches both ends. (Run machine back and forth or use the 'stitch tie off' button). Remove pins.

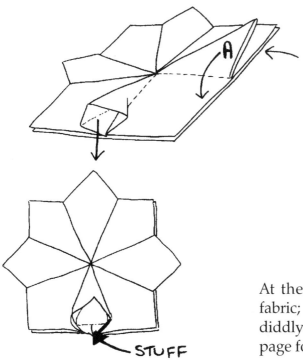

4. This block is totally double-sided and on both sides and in each of the corners there is a little flap - **A**. Lift the **A** flaps up; open and squash; press to remove the crease (made by ironing squares in half). Lo and behold here is a little pocket. This can be stuffed. If you turn the piece over, the back is the same as the front - it has little pockets as well - it's magic! You can stuff both sides.

At the corners there are two layers of fabric; tuck both in and here is another diddly pocket. Guess what! Turn over the page for the next exciting instalment.

You can stuff this as well, insert a folded square or anything else you fancy, and and and the edges roll!!! This is _really_ exciting.

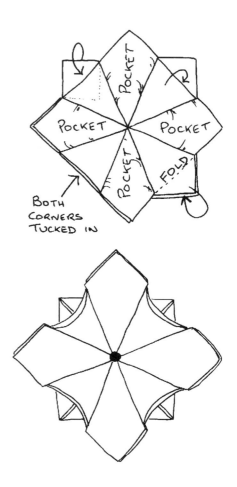

Stitch the new pockets down through all the layers. To complete the shape, turn any raw edges under and slipstitch. Enhance the centre with a button!

To be serious for a moment this silly 'Doofah' has lots of possibilities. You could stuff it with pot pourri, dried lentils or sawdust depending on the final use for the object. Make it out of metallic materials for a glittery Christmas decoration.

What about a 'Doofah' in different colours? To achieve this fascinating option you will have to cut lots more squares - sixteen in total.

### Make a 15"(38cm) Multicoloured Doofah Cushion

1. From four contrasting colours cut four sets of four 8"(20cm) squares (i.e. 16 squares in total). Arrange in a pleasing combination. Sew together to form _four identically coloured_ squares pressing all seams open and flat. Fold in half diagonally - _fold each one identically_. Interlock as before in stage 1 (page 37).

Sew across the block from one side to the other and top to bottom as previously described. There is no need to rule lines as you can follow the seams. Open out the flaps - and there is a lovely multicoloured 'Doofah'. Stuff all the pockets and turn the corners under and the raw edges in. Stitch through all the layers to secure. Do with it what you will - nicely of course!! P.S. Can you spot the mistake?

# Four-Pointed Flower

Imagine the woods in springtime with delicate violets shyly emerging from the mossy under-carpet. Birds calling sweetly to their tender young. The scent of daffodils and primroses gently wafting in the light spring breeze, their dainty petals dancing in the wispy air and lifting to the dappled sunshine. (Doesn't one write some rubbish!) I can remember meandering through these romantic woods with an absolutely smashing guy. This one flew quite literally into my life. His advert wasn't particularly riveting but 'any port in a storm', so I wrote off yet again - same letter but angled towards his comments on running, flying and playing music and his need for a quick-witted woman. You can imagine the waffle - flying round the countryside whilst blowing my own trumpet. (Rereading these letters fours years on I am totally surprised that anyone ever replied since the typing was riddled with mistakes, the grammar appalling and the layout truly disgusting. Most people would say 'What's new?'.) Anyway, he duly responded with a totally delightful letter mainly inquiring why I was apparently about to take a bungy jump (photo sent of me on bridge) and did the long skirt hide the wooden leg? This missive also informed me that he had all his own organs (including legs), but a personality disorder that required constant supplies of frozen strawberry yoghurt at unusual times. He said that he would fly down to a local airstrip to meet me. Well - love at first scan!! (Interesting to note that his typing was as bad as mine - good - we had something in common.)

So there I was waiting in the field, little plane hoves into sight, lands, door opens and he says 'Jump in' and I did. It then occurred to me that I was now in a plane miles up in the air with a total stranger - foolish woman - what could happen? Nothing. He needed both hands to fly the plane and I was completely safe - bit sad really because he looked very nice. Anyway we had a truly delightful day, lovely lunch and a splendid saunter through the woods. In addition to being charming, he baked his own bread (most impressed), flew his own plane (even more impressed) and ran marathons (really impressed). That was it - the man for me - he had all the things I really liked. We arranged to meet again, and in the intervening time I started breadmaking and took up running (flying lessons were too expensive and I'm not that mad).

At the end of the week I was puffing less and the rubbish bin was full of sad, flat, burnt and tasteless attempts at producing the perfect loaf. Sadly he called and said that he had thought about it and I was not the right one for him, so I wept a little, threw the running shorts in the bin and went to the supermarket for a decent bit of bread! Next day being Saturday, bought the paper and started again.

## Four-Pointed Flower

(photo previous page)

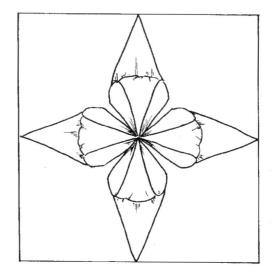

This block can be made from one main background material and four different colours for the petals or any other combination that you prefer.

Minimum quantity of fabric required for total block in 1 colour:

13"(33cm) x 44"(115cm)

### Prepare the Pieces

1. Use the rotary cutter and ruler to cut the following squares or make card templates; draw round and cut out.

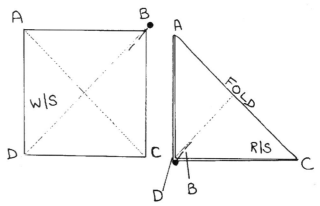

*For Four-Pointed Flower cut:*

Four 6"(15cm) squares for the petals (textured sections)

Four 6¾"(17cm) squares from the background material

2. Fold and press the petal squares (R/S out) on both diagonal lines. Lightly pencil the letters in all corners and on both sides (W/S & R/S) to help with the folding instructions. Lay flat, W/S up; *insert pin at B*. Bring **B** (with pin) corner to **D** (fold diagonally between **A/C**) as in the above diagram. Take **B** to **C** forming two folds at **C**: **D** and **A** touch. Select the **A** corner and fold over to **B/C** - three folds at **A/B/C** (pin in the middle). A 'quarter square' triangle is now constructed with three folds one end and only one at the other. (The pin is used to help identify which corner to move.) Press all these folds ensuring that they are exactly aligned. Carefully pin the layers together.

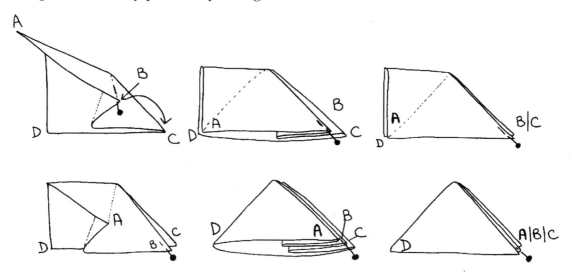

40

## Start Stitching

### *Use $^3/_8$"(1cm) seam allowance*

1. Baste - start from the folded end **E** and baste to the other end as in the diagram; keeping the stitching inside the $^3/_8$"(1cm) S/A. There are quite a lot of layers. To prevent all the layers sliding apart as you insert under the presser foot - *try lowering the feed dogs before insertion; remember to raise them again afterwards!* Lowering the feed dogs prevents the teeth from catching in all the layers; in addition the extra space created under the presser foot makes it much easier to position the shape.

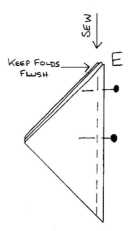

Berninas and many of the more 'mature' machines are very good at this little wheeze (feed dog lever is most convenient); if unable to perform this trick - just take care as you baste all the folds. Naturally, this manoeuvre can always be done by hand! *Baste with the longest stitch length - it has to be removed.*

2. Take two of the background squares; lay the basted shape on to one of the squares; align all the raw edges and position with the **three** folded end flush with the top right hand corner of the square (see below); pin carefully. Place the other square on top and sew seam. *Use $^3/_8$" seam allowance\*\*, stitch length as normal.* The textured shape is now trapped in between the two background squares. Remove basting and open the seams as much as possible. Opening the seams eases the excessive bulk - leaving the seam closed to one side makes a hefty ridge. { \*\*$^3/_8$" *is often marked on the throat plate under the presser foot (particularly on the older machines); if not, try moving the needle to the left hand side of the presser foot (away from the main body of machine) then use the inner edge of the presser foot as usual.*}

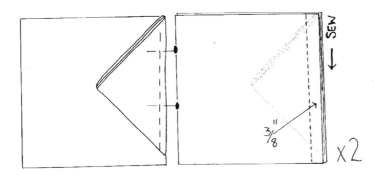

3. Repeat the last stage with a further folded petal and the last two background squares. There are still two folded shapes left.

4. Position the remaining shapes on to one of these pieces. Ensure that both folded triangles overlap each other and 'snuggle up' beside the previously inserted section. *This overlap will be at the precise spot where the previously textured insertion disappears into the seam.* Check this carefully - be picky at this point or the pieces may not all meet in the middle. (Remember - buttons are brill!!) Pin the pieces well and baste (Fig. 1 on next page).

Start basting just before the crucial centre point to prevent the pieces moving (starting at beginning of seam can result in the bits sliding before you reach the vital part). *Keep the basting within $^3/_8$"(1cm) seam allowance.*

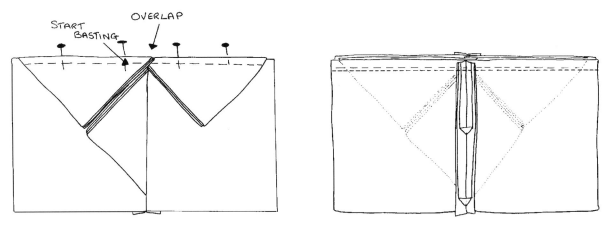

Fig. 1                                    Fig. 2

5. Lay the remaining section on top - turning its inserted section in the opposite direction away from the previously interposed one; match up the centre points; pin well. Stitch across the seam; use a larger needle and increase the normal stitch length slightly. *Thick layers/fabrics require a fatter/larger (14/90) needle to permit the machine to pierce through. The stitch length sometimes contracts on sewing through many layers as the feed dogs have difficulty in pulling such a thickness).* Some people prefer to start around the middle of the seam to prevent the points sliding or you can sew from one side to the other. The seam should be $^3/_8$"; but more importantly ensure that you sew through the junction of all the points, or a covered button will be in order.

Remove basting and press open all the seams as much as possible. Block should measure 12½"(31cm) square; trim to this measurement but leave if only a fraction smaller - giving the block a good tug can usually persuade it to fit other sections of the quilt. (Good technical advice!)

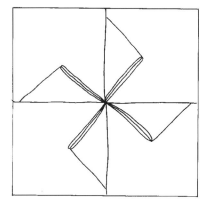

6. Now you can play. Fiddle, twiddle and flatten the textured portions in which ever way you fancy.

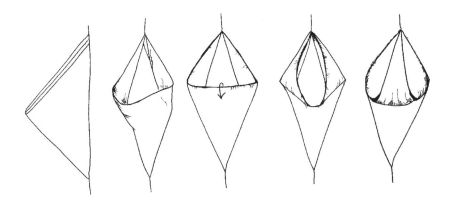

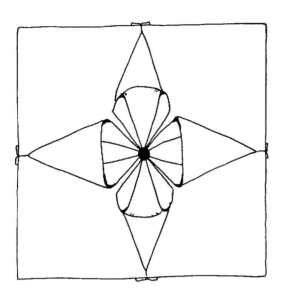

7. Different designs may be made by manipulating the textured shape in alternate ways.

Why not experiment with two inserted one way up and two the other?

*Should a slight glitch/hitch have occurred in the centre you can always -*

**Jazz up the Junction!!**

*Covered buttons are ace* for concealing any minor muddles in the centre, alternatively you could be frightfully frivolous and freak out with a fanciful flower. This little natty notion is ideal for masking tiny problems and will add a soupçon of embellishment and extra decoration.

## Feathery Fringed Flowers

This is a well-known 'free machine embroidery' technique and is not difficult to make. Try it but if you find the thought too terrifying then get a button or stop fussing. (No one will notice any diminutive deviations - we can be far too pernickety when assessing our work. This is not an excuse for shoddy workmanship so if any junction is really bad you should unpick and re-stitch, or I suppose go and get an extra large button!)

### Free machine embroidery

This is an intriguing skill that has been developed by some artists to a amazingly high level. Using the machine for this creative art form involves lowering/covering the feed dogs (serrated teeth under the presser foot), playing with the top and bottom thread tension and learning a good degree of control! Don't panic - do try this effect just for a bit of fun. The next sections will proffer a few basic rules and suggestions that will help tremendously.

First basic rule is to sit comfortably and relax!! This is meant to be a fun experience not a tense battle of wills. The machine is your friend, not a big bad ogre (although sometimes it seems this way) - learn to love it! Also, it will help to have a comfortable sitting posture. Sit properly at the machine - do not hunch your shoulders or have them tensely up under your ears! Try to sit a little further away, with your bottom poking out; push the machine away from you a little and get your elbows on the table; resting your body weight on the elbows leaves the hands and wrists free to manipulate the material. Raising or lowering your chair seat can also help. Tilting the machine slightly towards you with a small flat slat of wood or thin book may help. This action enables one to see the working area around the needle more clearly.

Second basic rule is to use a darning/free embroidery/hopper foot on the machine (special presser foot that does not touch the base plate when presser foot lever lowered). This is free-machining, and as you are going to control and manoeuvre the fabric the presser foot must not sit firmly on the material: should it do so you will not be able to rotate the work. It is possible to create machine embroidered effects with no presser foot at all and/or with a spring needle (special type), but I have always found that using the darning foot makes everything much easier. It is a little safer as the metal loop does protect the fingers a wee bit more. (If you are wondering why the foot is sometimes referred to as a 'hopper' foot, then the explanation is very simple - as you run the machine the foot bounces (hops): often one is not aware of this, but once the foot is in place just run the machine and see.)

The feed dogs (serrated teeth) need to be lowered or covered with a plate - see the instruction book for details. If the teeth can't be lowered/covered then it may not be possible to do this type of embroidery. Older machines frequently have a knob or dial on the top or side which controls the pressure on the presser foot - turn this to its lowest point; now there will be virtually no pressure under the foot - check your instruction manual to ensure that you have turned the correct dial. Pfaff owners will need to remember that most of their machines have a two-stage presser foot lever and it has to be at the first stage (latched into a little shelf), then enough space remains under the presser foot to permit free movement of the work.

Generally speaking in machine embroidery, a larger, heavier and stronger needle is required to pierce through the many layers of built up thread. Incidentally it is very easy to break the needles when doing this, so lay in a few spare. Special needles are now available with a longer groove above the eye (reputed to lead to fewer breakages or less fraying on using metallic or other difficult threads).

Finally, your choice of thread is important. To begin with, use the same type of thread from the same manufacturer, preferably polyester with a 40 count. Threads vary tremendously in thickness; often there will be a number on the reel such as 30, 40 or 50 (higher thread count = thinner thread). Polyester thread is stronger than cotton but you may find that the machine will perform better with cotton thread. Cotton and silk are natural fibres and consequently inert; man-made threads create a degree of static which can sometimes affect the stitch performance of certain machines. It is well worth experimenting with different types and construction of thread to discover which make the machine prefers. Learn the technique before you rush out and buy the wonderful embroidery threads that are available nowadays.

To make Feathery Fringed flowers you will need:
Darning/free embroidery/hopper foot + 8" (20cm) wooden embroidery hoop
10"(25cm) square of firmly woven scrap fabric such as calico or sheeting.
90/100 (14/16) machine needle + selection of threads - polyester, cotton or silk

1. Insert the fabric into the hoop. Pull firmly to ensure that it is drum tight. The fabric which will contain the embroidery has to be inserted into a hoop of some description to keep it taut. Omitting to do this either ends up with the material firmly stuck through the throat plate or the embroidered cloth becomes very

distorted. I find that a wooden embroidery hoop is an essential - ***bind the inner rim of the hoop with some old bias tape or strips of cloth*** - this will grip the fabric much better and cause less damage to the base material. It is considerably easier to get the fabric taut in a bound wooden hoop than certain other plastic/metal ones, although some people do favour these.

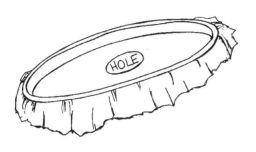

2. Draw a circle: 1½″ (3 - 4cm) in diameter. ***CUT OUT leaving a HOLE***. Check that the feed dogs are lowered or covered; darning foot in place. Stitch length and width should be at **0** (good working practice). Top and bottom thread tensions at normal. Put the hoop under the needle (you may have to push the presser foot shank up a little to slide it under); have the fabric in the bottom of the hoop (the inner hoop visible).

3. Position the needle ¼″ (0.5cm) from the hole (above the fabric). Bring the lower bobbin thread to the top of the fabric - more good working practice and prevents the bottom thread getting entangled underneath. Lower presser foot; hold top thread firmly; lower needle through fabric; raise needle and hook up the bottom bobbin thread. Hold these threads securely while you do a few stitches on the spot. Cut threads off.

4. Running the machine slowly but moving the hoop fairly quickly, sew directly across the hole (North - South) on to the other side stopping ¼″ (.5cm) into the cloth. Staying at this distance from the hole, stitch to West - East and sew across the opening again. Repeat at the other intersections of the circle forming eight sections (Fig. 1).

Figs. 1 - 3

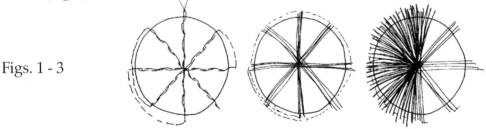

5. Sew several more times across the circle at these points (Fig. 2) - keep crossing through the centre and sewing ¼″ (0.5cm) into the surrounding cloth. Try to keep the hoop moving fairly rapidly in comparison to the machine. Running the machine fast and moving the work slowly makes tightly locked stitching - best flowers are made by lightly 'locked' stitching which will unravel on completion to produce nicely fringed shapes. Bit like rubbing tummy and patting head - very hard to run ***machine slowly*** and move ***hoop quickly***.

6. Fill in the circle (Fig. 3) by sewing from the edge to the centre and back (similar to the spokes of a wheel). Do ensure that you lock the stitching into the centre. Some embroidery manuals suggest that you keep sewing across the entire circle (from one side to the other) but I find that this gets exceptionally thick with packed threads and just as good an effect can be achieved by sewing edge to centre and back.

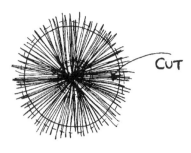

CUT

7. Continue stitching until the circle is totally filled. The more lines you stitch means the more feathery the flower; less gives a slightly anorexic effect! Sew into the centre, and running the machine fast and moving the hoop slowly, sew several times round the periphery of the centre to lock all the threads. This will make very small stitches which will hold all the layers of thread together. Stitch back on to the fabric. Cut the flower out, keeping as close to the fabric as possible.

8. Make another one in the same way. The hole is re-usable! Change the colours of the top and bottom threads. Having made one more, don't cut it out; leave in the fabric; draw and cut a smaller or little larger hole elsewhere on the fabric and make a further one. The base fabric can be used lots of times for different sized flowers, but do not have more than one hole at any one time or it will weaken the tautness of the material.

How about using up all the old threads and having varicoloured flowers? In fact you could plaster the work with these little florets and everyone would think you had been so clever and not merely mucked up a few junctions.

# Eight Petal Flower

I have had great difficulty in thinking of wondrously original titles for these textured blocks. It was much easier to find a nickname for some of the gentlemen I met. For instance there was Alf the Australian who was a contact from the local paper. I had a salutary lesson when I ventured into the Personal columns of the aforesaid rag. Up to this point all my dates from the 'Times' had been with extremely nice, albeit a trifle odd (but aren't we all?) and well-behaved gentlemen. I only tried a different avenue because that week there wasn't any likely-looking talent in the 'Times'. In the local paper you can ring a number and listen to their voice before you decide whether or not to leave a message. That's quite interesting purely as an exercise by itself. Anyway I left a couple of messages for two gentlemen and waited. The first response proved to be someone who was seeking a little on the side. Sorry - that is definitely not for me. The second caller sounded O.K. so we agreed to meet. Well!!!! I am quite glad that I can run quite quickly. This was one of those rare times when a hasty exit is necessary - all 'our' Alf was interested in was 'Down-Under' and I'm not playing that game. Certainly not in a car!!! I returned home with my tail tucked very firmly between my legs and vowed not to repeat that experiment again. Needless to say he phoned several times and I had to be quite nasty to make him realise that I was not interested at all.

Now Eager Eddy was another kettle of fish. A dear little chap with delightful manners and totally charming. The snag was that I do not 'go' for men who are shorter than I am. He took a real big shine to me, constantly ringing up and sending flowers, small presents would arrive in the post and I hadn't the heart to tell him that he was wasting his time. Fortunately, he was a Bridge fanatic and there, I failed him. Bridge and I do not mix. We went to several Bridge evenings; he offered to teach me how to play it on the computer using his special programme. (Golly, I can barely use the word processor let alone try to play Bridge.) In the end I had to pluck up the courage and tell him that I didn't think that I could possibly 'bridge' the gap between us and that it had to stop. He still remained hopeful and left endearing messages on the answer-phone. This became very embarrassing when the latest bod who'd come back for a meal and to meet the child, helpfully zaps the button for me to hear the messages!! Egg-on-face time again and this one never returned after that evening. Pity, but he was called 'Ethelred the Unready' and I'm not telling you why!

So we had Pompous Pat, Manic Martin, Dandy David and Roger the Dodger in addition to Diffident Daniel to name but a few. Goodness knows what names I collected. Jaundiced Jenifer or Raddled Rayment may have featured among the choices. I can even remember being introduced at a party by one man as his 'Floosie'! Now I'm perfectly happy to be known as the 'Bide-a-while'.

## Eight Petal Flower (photo on page 4)

This block is brilliant in colour. Why not try two complementary tones or use contrasting hues? Use up scraps and create a multi-shaded Flower. Make a note of the desired colour scheme then refer to the plan as you stitch. It's amazing how many times the gremlins move the colours out of order.

Minimum quantity of fabric required to make total block in 1 colour:

17"(45cm) x 44"(115cm)

### Prepare the Pieces

1. Use the rotary cutter and ruler to cut the following squares and rectangles or make card templates; draw round and cut out.

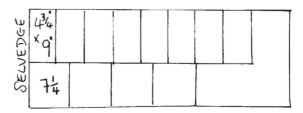

*To make the petals cut:*
Eight rectangles 4¾"(12cm) x 9"(23cm)
Use a combination of colours if desired.

*From the background material cut:*
Four 7¼"(18cm) squares

### Start Stitching - (S/A ³⁄₈"(1cm) unless stated )

1. Fold all rectangles in half lengthways, *R/S on inside*. Stitch down one side; use normal stitch length and ¼"(0.5cm) seam; sew from raw edges towards fold. Gently press the seam open - to do this open and flatten the shape (forming a triangle) - try not to press the sides of the triangle yet. Clip off corner and turn R/S out; poke corner out gently. Carefully press into a triangular shape.

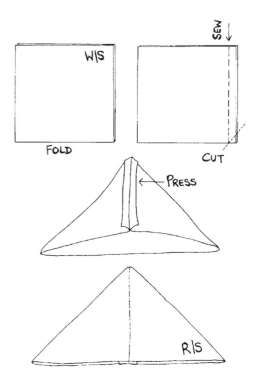

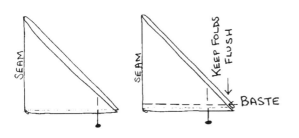

2. Refold all these sections in half forming a smaller triangle; keep *seam* on the outside as in diagram. Pin layers keeping the two folds flush. Baste the raw edges together. There are now eight little 'sandwiches'.

48

3. Cut all four background squares diagonally in half forming eight triangles. Take two of these triangles; place one 'sandwich' on the bias edge, align all raw edges, position 'sandwich' $3/_8$"(1cm) down from the top (as in diagram). Pin in place. Position the second triangle on top, and stitch $3/_8$"(1cm) seam down the bias edge. This 'sandwich' is now inserted diagonally in the square. Trim off 'ears'. Remove basting; lightly press seam open taking care not to crease the

'sandwich'. Repeat this action **3 times** making **four squares** with the 'sandwiches' in them. There are four basted shapes still remaining. *Should your sample fail to resemble the diagram just twist the 'sandwich' over.*

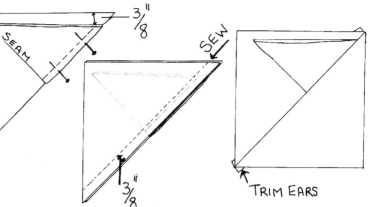

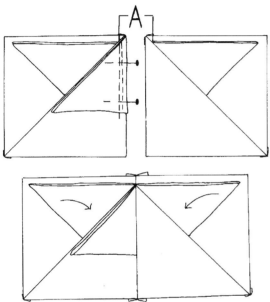

4. Take two of these squares and one 'sandwich'; position as shown in left hand drawing aligning all raw edges; ensure the 'sandwich' is touching the first inserted one at **A**; pin and baste to prevent movement. Lay the next square on top matching the points at **A** (R/S together); stitch down side using $3/_8$"(1cm) seam, endeavouring to sew through **A**. Remove basting and gently press the seam open.

Repeat with the remaining two squares: there are now two sets of squares with three textural inserts and *two 'sandwiches' left*.

5. *Turn shapes towards centre and pin down or they will 'catch' in the next seam.* Position last pair of 'sandwiches' as shown in the diagram on to one of these sets. *Overlap at A.* Pin well, baste to secure. Start basting at the centre - sew to one end, then reverse work and complete the line. Take the second set of squares and place R/Ss together, lining all the **A** points in the centre; pin, baste if preferred; sew this last seam.

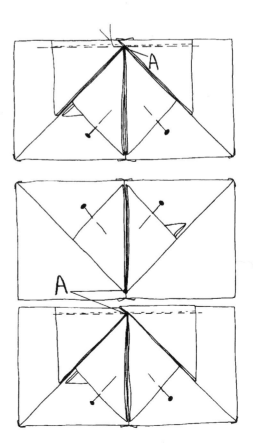

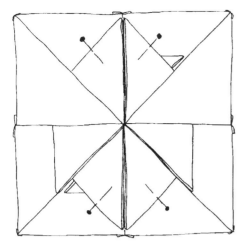

Open out. On completion press the last seam open and trim any excess bulk from the pieces if desired. Ironing the compacted centre where all the seams meet is jolly good for cleaning the bottom of the iron!!! Manipulate the shapes by gently pulling the ends apart, thus extending the width and making the 'sandwich' easy to flatten. *PS Covered buttons are really effective or Feathery Flowers (page 44 to 46)!*

## Developing the Design

Experiment with rolling and twisting the edges. Manipulate the flaps back and forth or fold over. Add beads or tassels to the points.

Fold every other shape flat (into a square), turn the edge back. Open out the others - see photograph below.

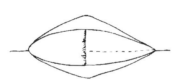

Insert the 'sandwich' into any seam. Have six in a hexagonal format; four in between squares or rectangles. Link side by side or in a row (end to end) for a border or as a textural insertion in a garment.

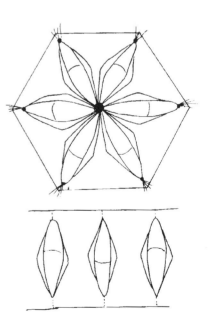

Sampler quilt (62" x 80")
(Reading from L-R)
Top row: Luscious Lilies, Stuffed Squares and Contrariwise Cathedral Window.
2nd row: Folded Fabrication, Driven Dotty and Four Pointed Flower.
3rd row: Multiple Origami Twist, Eight Petal Flower and Puffball block.
4th row: Trumpets, Stuffed Squares and Trumpets.
5th row: Corners on Log Cabin, Textured Star and Tucked Up Fan.
Made from calico & silk, machine pieced & hand quilted.
(Midge Pitter).

'Not just Calico' - random sized textured blocks with some machine trapunto, machine pieced & quilted. (Shelagh Jarvis).

'Nine Patch' (46" x 46") - Tucked Up Fans & patchwork blocks, machine pieced & quilted. (Jennie Rayment).

'Blue Flower' (32" x 32") - patchwork blocks with a border of Interlocked Squares, machine pieced & quilted. (Jennie Rayment).

'Revolution' (28" x 30") - constructed from hand stitched Fancy Fandangoes, hand pieced & applied to background, machine quilted. (Jennie Rayment).

# Tucked Up Fan

Now for a little 'Nipping and Tucking' in a sort of circular fashion. Life seems to go in circles with various forays up other avenues then back to the usual daily round. It's the little deviations that make life interesting. I have to admit that I enjoyed my little explorations into the man-hunting maze. Before one could even select which chap to meet, you had to understand the rather cryptic nature of the adverts.

Gentleman-seeking is a bit like buying a house. It's what is missing from the advert that counts or the somewhat misleading wording. For instance when you see a house described as 'deceptively spacious' this frequently means 'pokey' (small). This applies to the adverts in the 'lonely hearts column'. Should the word 'tall' be omitted then the guy concerned is very small; the word 'Christian' attached, then the guy is very religious; his age left out then he is way past his sell-by-date, and so on. If they leave out the area where they live then you can read 'absolutely desperate will go anywhere' or perhaps they live in the Outer Hebrides where no right-thinking girl will go for the evening. Their interests can be revealing too: interest in opera equals really boring; interest in walking and golf means you are the caddie while he plays golf; interest in athletics will mean long distance running; interest in football - forget it! But an interest in gymnastics could be interesting!!!

Then there are the abbreviations: N/S means 'non-smoking' not 'near-sighted' or 'no sex': ALA is 'all letters answered' (they don't) not 'absolute liar always': OH/OC is not 'or hot or cold' but 'own house/own car': GSOH does not mean 'great sex on holiday' but 'great sense of humour': TLC refers to the fact that he is a 'totally lascivious chap': WLTM means 'would like to meet' and not 'wouldn't last 'till morning'! There are other phrases such as a liking for food and wine which can be translated as overweight, drunken and debauched, and if he says he's 'hot-blooded' watch it!! (Initials can be very misleading especially when you are travelling. I usually stay in hotels or boarding houses (not people's houses) and I have never yet found a B & B (booze and bonking) to live up to its promise).

Finally there are the picky ones who are after a specific something like the chap who wanted someone of 'notable proportions', who had to be of a certain size and weight. Amazingly I was the exact height and weight but as I explained in my letter was not of notable proportions because I wasn't very large. It transpired that he was after a 'dolly bird' with a large chest. The notable proportions referred to cup size and not to being an Amazonian of a woman. He wanted 'D' cups and all I have is egg-cups!!!

## Tucked - Up Fan (photo on page 57)

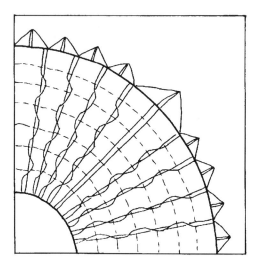

The more astute amongst you will promptly realise that this is a direct lift from the 'Tucked Up Circle' featured in the previous books. It is a very useful block for the corners of your quilt, and creates a pleasing arc which rather nicely complements the overall design. Join four together to form a circular design, or make several and create a series of curves.

Minimum fabric required for total block in one colour: 16"(40cm) x 44"(115cm)

### Prepare the Pieces

1. Use the rotary cutter and ruler to cut the following squares or make paper templates (use newspaper or brown paper for economy). Pin in place, draw round and cut out. *Trace the template* for the base of the fan and the 'degree marking' pattern (*exactly as shown in the text on page 108*). *Caution - photocopying is not always accurate - the 1:1 relationship can be out of synch.*

*To make the Fan cut:*
One 15½"(38cm) square + One Template B (page 108)
*From the background material cut:*
One 12½"(31cm) square

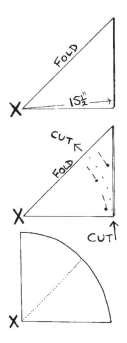

2. Fold the 15½"(38cm) square in half diagonally and press. Measure 15½"(38cm) from the corner **X** and make small mark - use a pencil. Continue measuring and marking until an arc of dots appears. Check that you measure from the corner each time and don't let the ruler wander elsewhere. Pin layers together. Cut through the arc; open out to reveal a quarter circle.

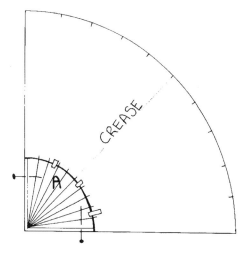

### Start Stitching

1. Place the tracing of template **A** on the corner (fabric R/S up), aligned with the raw edges. The midpoint of the template should match the pressed crease - don't panic if it doesn't quite! Pin and tape in place. *Draw round the arc first.* (Template is drawn in imperial measurements but may be used for any metric designs.)

2. A long ruler will be useful at this juncture. Position the ruler so it bisects the corner of template and is exactly coordinated with the drawn lines; mark the *outer edge* of template with a small dash and the inner edge of the quarter circle. Repeat until you have made nine little dashes round both curved edges. Cut through the drawn arc line (follow the pencil line) removing the entire corner. *Do not cut off all the little marks*.

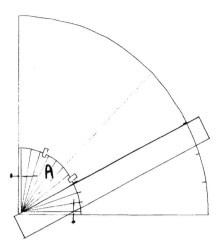

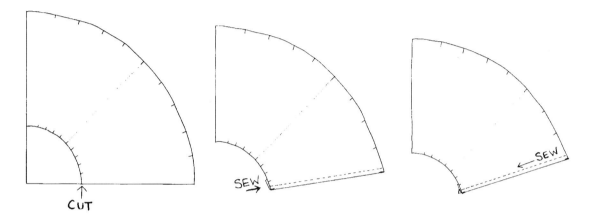

3. Fold on the first set of marks, R/S out. Sew with a ¼"(0.5cm) seam from this fold as in diagram. Use thread matched to fabric. Repeat on the next three sets of marks. There will now be four tucks radiating out. Alternate the direction of the stitching up then down to prevent distortion.

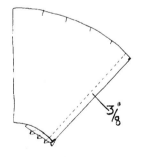

4. *At the fifth set (centre) sew a larger seam - ³/₈"(1cm).* Repeat as for stage 4 for the remaining four sets of marks {¼"(0.5cm) seam}. You will now have nine tucks - eight of equal size and the centre one larger. *Press the centre tuck flat*. Insert a thin bias bar - a flat slat or knitting needle will aid the process. Press the tucks on either side towards the central flattened one, as shown in the drawings.

*DOUBLE, DOUBLE check that you use the correct set of marks (ones that are diametrically opposite each other). Failure to do this results in UNPICKING. If preferred you can stitch the centre ³/₈"(1cm) first, then sew the others: this cuts down the margin for error.*

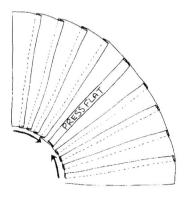

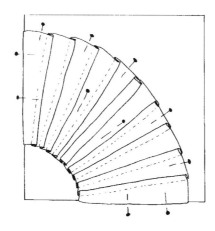

5. Lay the tucked section W/S down on to the background square. Do not panic if does not quite fit - jiggle it a bit to make it fit as best as possible. The most important thing is to have it sitting fully on the background square - don't fuss if a bit hangs off. This can always be trimmed later. Pin the layers carefully together.

6. Take the fabric template **B** as previously cut out and the paper one. *Cut through the dotted line on the paper one <u>only</u>* - (reduces the arced edge by ¼"(.5cm). Place the paper template on the W/S of the  fabric template **B**; align the straight sides; pin. Preferably by hand, baste the excess fabric around the arc to the paper template, clipping and pleating the excess fullness for a perfect outline; press the basted edge. Keep knots on the R/S - makes them easier to remove. Or you could simply fold the arced edge over the template and press but sometimes little glitches occur and you'll get a lumpy silhouette. You may prefer to machine round the paper arc marking the curve with stitch before turning the fabric over.

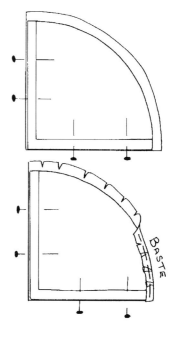

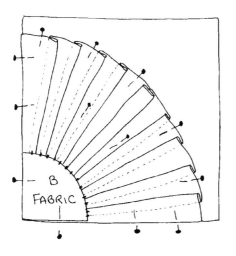

7. Position the fabric covered template **B** on to the Tucked Up segment. Baste in place. Attach the arced edge by hand hem/slip stitching or use the Blind Hem stitch on the machine (see page 29 for more detail). Sew through all the layers. Remove the basting; pull out the paper; lift the fabric and trim off any excess from the pleated portion - trim to ¼"(.5cm) S/A. <u>**Do not cut the backing fabric**</u>.

8. Now for a bit of fun. We can play!! Notice use of the royal 'we' - what I really mean is...........................*You* can play.

## Twiddling the Tucks

The tucks can now be twisted for maximum dynamic interest. (Wow!) Measure 1"(2.5cm) from the applied arc section and make a series of light dots on the tucks; use a pencil. These dots will be concealed when the tucks are twisted. Sew round on these marks turning (twisting) the tucks in the reverse direction as you go; twist four tucks one way, keeping the central one flat, and twist four tucks the other way. Measure again for the next round of stitches; take the measurements from the applied arc edge at all times. This will ensure that all the rows will remain truly parallel to this arced section. Although the most accurate, this method can be time-consuming.

Achieve the same effect with the Quilting Guide. This 'L' shaped piece slots, clips or screws on to some part of the presser foot. Many machines have this small part in the box of attachments, but it is not expensive to buy if you do not possess one.

Set the desired measurement between the edge of the guide and the machine needle. The trick is to follow the last line of stitching (round the edge of the applied arc) with the tip of the lever thus sewing an exact replica of the arc but 1"(2.5cm) away. This is considerably speedier but you have to sew all the lines in an anti-clockwise (counter-clockwise U.S.A.) direction rather than the usual clockwise which feels a little awkward; in addition accuracy is paramount as you can only follow the previously stitched line and not the original one.

Continue with either method, twisting and turning the tucks as displayed in the diagrams, until you reach 1"(2.5cm) approximately from the outer edge.

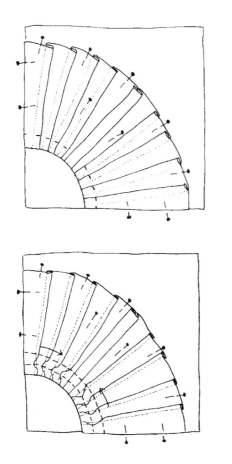
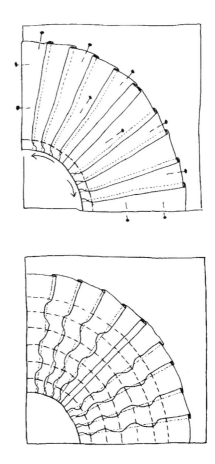

## Fancy Twiddling

Who says that the measurements have to be at equal spacing? Why not change the distances between the rows? What about some decorative stitching instead of straight? Try the effect of some lace, ribbon or cord couched on to the stitching, or different coloured threads. Go on - experiment!

## Completing the Edge

Carefully fold the raw edge under by approximately ¼"(0.5cm). Check that it is parallel to the last row of stitching. A sneaky trick is to measure the distance between the last line of stitching and the desired place to fold the fabric under. Lightly mark this measurement all the way round and fold under on the marks. If preferred machine round the marked arc, but fold back the backing fabric first. Pin and baste the folded edge.

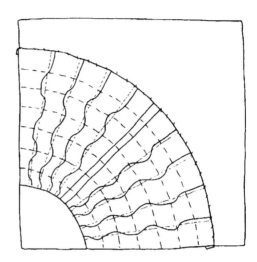

For a plain edge - just hand slip/hem stitch down through all the layers. For a decorative edge - tuck lace under and stitch down or insert a few folded squares.

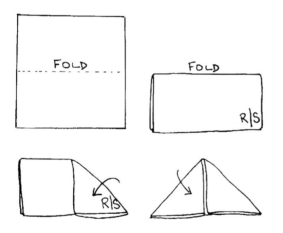

I like using the Somerset (British) or Sharkstooth (USA) method of folding. To decide on the size of the folded squares; measure the distance between the twisted tucks, add ½"(1cm) seam allowance; fold as in the diagram. Tuck under the edge of the fan. Wiggle them until they appear evenly spaced and of equal height; pin in place; sew round the edge through all the layers.

If preferred there is nothing to stop you binding the raw edge of the fan and then stitching down. Add some lace, braid or even a frill to enhance the appearance.

## Final Fandango

As there are two layers of fabric at the corner of the fan, padding could always be inserted to make a raised and stuffed base for the fan. Decorative lines of embroidery could be added to make the 'ribs' complete. How about using a thick embroidery silk stitching the lines and leaving long ends, then tying the ends to form a tassel as in the photograph of a fancy fan?

**<u>Twiddled,</u>**
**<u>Fiddled</u>**
**<u>& Padded</u>**
**<u>Fancy Fan</u>**

The Tucked Up Fan closely resembles a traditional patchwork called Drunkards Path featured in many quilting books. There are several different ways to utilise the this pattern; why not remake some of these designs substituting the fan block for the other? Experiment with your own innovative layout.

Think about miniaturising or enlarging the fan block. Reduce the outer arced edge of the **A** template for a smaller version; extend the lines, redraw the outer arced edge for a larger one. Explore the effect of flattening/squashing all the tucks, or change the twisting pattern.

**Have a little play. Life is <u>meant</u> to be fun!!**

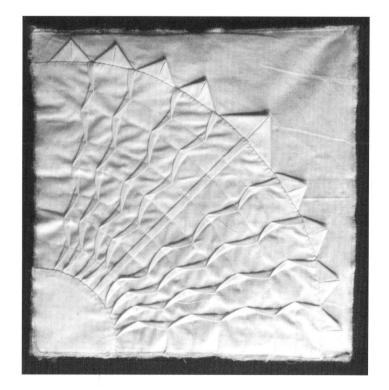

# Textured Star

So called because there is a certain amount of fullness in the centre when you complete the design. This appears to be a problem with many people these days - a undeniable degree of fullness around the middle. It's very comfy on a cold winter night but not so good when you are forced to share a hammock, and useless on a seesaw. I do seem to attract gentlemen with a nicely contoured corpulence.

One of my little adventures involved a most delightful chappie who was a driving instructor and his proportions were truly notable. His passions were wining, dining and dancing. Dancing was the problem. You had to bend around the contour and decide whether to stand on tiptoe and be above or bend your knees and be below. If above and clutched to his chest I was very aware that my feet were not always on the ground, thus presenting a somewhat ridiculous sight - the legs twitching desperately above the floor in a vain attempt to find a toehold. He was into gambling as well - did you know that you should always play the fruit machines by the door as they give better results? Roulette and blackjack should always be played between 6.00 p.m. and 7.00 p.m. because the House gives preferable odds. These moves are designed to entice you further into the den of iniquity to play other machines where the odds are less well favoured, or persuade you to return later bringing all your friends to play the gaming tables; and they don't tell you that they 'up the ante'. Nevertheless, he did teach me how to do handbrake turns.

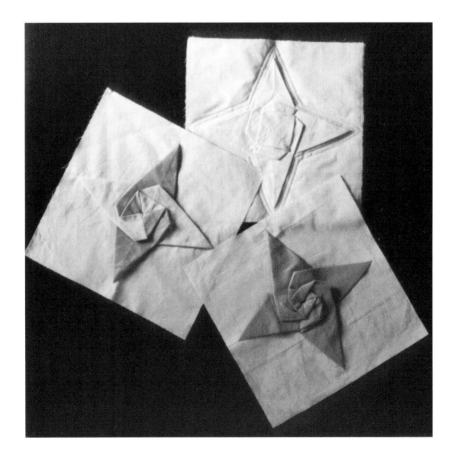

## Textured Star (photo on previous page)

The actual Star part is constructed from four squares which could all be different colours. It is then inserted into the background fabric. Decide on how many colours to use.

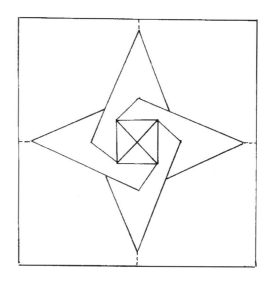

Minimum quantity of fabric required for total block in one colour:
13"(33cm) x 44"(115cm)

### Prepare the Pieces

1. Use the rotary cutter and ruler to cut the following squares; or make card templates, lay on and draw round, and cut out.

*For the Textured Star cut:* four 6"(14cm) squares - select one to four colours.
*(The metric version is slightly smaller than the imperial one unless you really wish to cut 14.5cm squares. Feel free to do so if desired).*

*From the background material cut:* four 6½"(16cm) squares

### Start Stitching

*All seam allowances ¼"(0.5cm)*

1. To make the actual Textured Star section lay out the four x 6"(14cm) squares in the selected correct colour arrangement. Stitch together to form a larger square, ***LEAVING the FIRST ¾"(2cm) of all the seams on the outer edge unsewn*** - leave a gap when you sew or unpick if you forget. Press all seams open and flat.

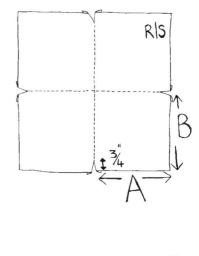

2. Keep the square *R/S out*. Fold one quarter in half diagonally aligning **A** side with **B** side, matching up raw edges. Repeat with the remaining three quarters as in the diagram. The square now resembles an upside-down pyramid. Baste these edges - use a long stitch length and keep the stitching within the ¼"(0.5cm) seam allowance. Sew the entire seam in each case.

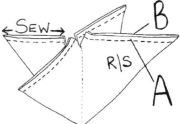

59

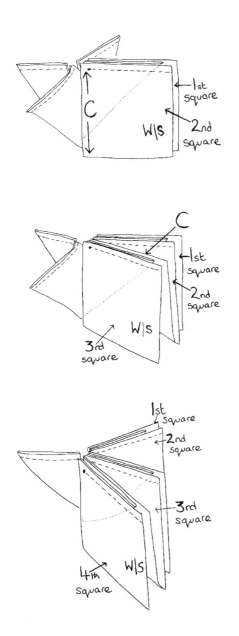

3. Select two of the background fabric squares, and isolate one of the four seams from the Textured Star section. Place one of these squares either side of the seam aligning all raw edges (sandwiching the seam), R/S together. Stitch using ¼"(0.5cm) seam but ***START THE SEAM ½"(1CM) IN FROM THE EDGE***. Stitch from the centre towards the outer edges.

4. Select the next seam (work systematically) and one more background square; place this square in front of the seam - use **C** side of the previously attached square from stage 3 for the back of the seam. Align the raw edges and sew - *remember to leave ½"(1cm) from the start of the seam*. Sew from the centre out. Repeat this technique with the next seam and remaining square.

5. The last seam is sandwiched by using the adjacent sides of the first and fourth attached background squares. Align the raw edges and sew, starting ¼"(0.5cm) in from the centre as shown below.

What you are trying to do is insert the Textured Star portion into the seam junctions of the other four squares. Leaving the first ½"(1 cm) unstitched enables the outer background squares to be rotated as you sew. Should you not understand these instructions then lay the four background squares out flat and place the Textured Star part on top, setting the seams of the Textured Star in between. 'You should now see what to do', says she hopefully. This piecing technique can be used when sewing the textural version of the Bow Tie patchwork (see '**Tucks Textures & Pleats**', page 74).

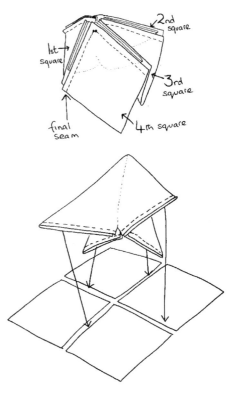

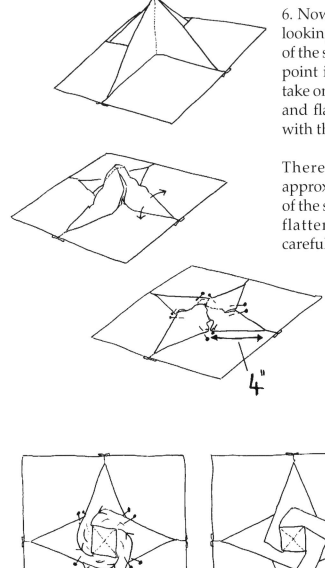

6. Now you have to turn that strange looking bag into a star. Pull the centre of the star up until it forms a point. The point is at the apex of four triangles; take one of the triangles and pull apart and flatten gently. Repeat this action with the remaining three triangles.

There is one particular spot approximately 4"(10cm) down the side of the squashed triangle where all four flattened shapes touch: pin this carefully to the background material.

Manipulate the remainder round in a clockwise fashion or maybe anti clockwise (counter clockwise U.S.A.), and with a bit of luck it will flatten as in the picture. If preferred you can 'scrunch' the centre by catching the excess in a variety of places through to the background fabric (see drawing below).

7. Press if necessary to maintain the pleats. Anchor the folds securely by hand wherever essential to maintain the shape.

Why not put a matching button in the centre or embellish with beads? There are several unusual ways to manipulate this design. Experiment with rolling edges or inserting other folded squares under parts of the textured shape. See what happens if you use stripes!

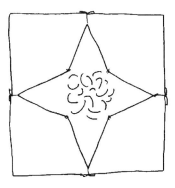

**Go on - fiddle and twiddle it a bit.**

# Multiple Origami* Twist

Here is a block that you can really wiggle, fiddle and jiggle to your heart's content. It reminds me of the guy with some very curious mannerisms including an uncontrollable urge to twiddle his beard. The advertisement sounded interesting - this one described himself as a BFG. which I gather stands for Big Friendly Giant not as I thought Booze and Food Gourmet. I wrote off the usual letter; he rang. He seemed just the ticket: tall, fair, obviously intelligent, interested in books and a farming background. His voice sounded pleasant so maybe this would be the one for me. We arranged to meet in a wine bar at the back of Sotheby's in London.

Out with the posh frock, on with the make-up and off on the train, scads of perfume - just in case. I was early but I thought that I would wait inside for him. Just inside the door was a guy who matched the description exactly. I plucked up courage and asked him if he was Mr. X? No. Quickly, hiding my blushes, I sat down before I got arrested for soliciting. No sign of the BFG, so I bought a glass of wine and waited. Finally, the man in question arrived carrying a wonderful Book of Hours that he had just purchased for £400 at Sotheby's. He bought himself a glass of vino and we chatted. It rapidly became apparent that he had a strange way of behaving; this involved twiddling his beard, tapping on the table and going 'Wheehee' every so often. I was fascinated. We chatted for an hour or so about his three houses, his farm, his bookshop and various other things, all of which was interspersed with various twiddles and 'Wheehees'. Suddenly, he leapt up from the table and asked if I had eaten? Instant quandary - do I really want to remain here? I was hungry and thought that I might at least get a meal out of him (mercenary woman). He inquired politely if I had an Underground travel ticket and with that we set off.

Down into the subway, three changes of train later, we arrived at an Indian vegetarian restaurant in a really salubrious area (Hmmm!). Looked a bit more like a bus station cafe. It was unlicensed, so next door I purchased the cider. We ate accompanied by twiddles and twitches and 'Wheehees'. I failed to eat much so he removed my plate and finished off mine. He asked me to share the bill - all of £13.42 (no wonder he has three houses!) and suggested that we returned homewards. The BFG. had to be back on the 10.15 pm train because his parking ticket ran out - he had no intention of making a night of it. Pondering over this in later years, I suspect that he considered me a little odd for not truly appreciating the cuisine (excellent to his taste; sticky rice, rancid greasy chickpeas in a orange curry goo with a bit of old blanket (naan bread) to mine). Diving back into the tube, we changed once, and just as we passed the third station, he jumped up, and cried 'I should have got off at the last station'. The train stopped and with a final twiddle and 'Wheehee' he vanished. I completed the journey by myself now feeling very sick with cider, Indian nosh and a glass of plonk swilling around. I didn't feel exactly brilliant the next day either. Moral - do not be swayed by the attractions of a  BFG.

*My apologies for the title of this block - it does sound a little peculiar.*

## Multiple Origami Twist
(photograph on page 65)

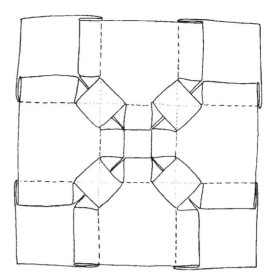

This is all one piece of material, but have a few scraps to hand as there are several places where a little bit can be tucked in or under. The M.O.T. may appear to be very complex but follow the diagrams carefully and see how simple it is, it's just complicated to describe. Don't give up - just try it. You may well amaze yourself!

Minimum quantity of fabric required to make the total block in one colour:
18"(48cm) x 44"(115cm)
(sufficient for two)

### Prepare the Pieces

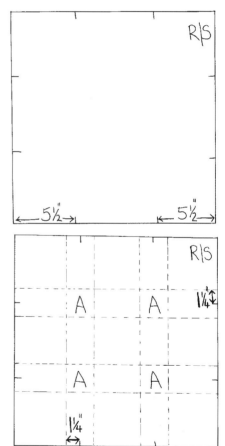

1. Use a rotary cutter and ruler to cut the following square or make a paper template (use newspaper). Pin in place, draw round and cut out.

*To make the Twist cut:*

One 17½"(43.5cm) square
*(Same size as Puffball (page 66) - save time - cut 2)*

2. Carefully measure 5½"(13.5cm) in from each corner and mark all outer edges of the square on the R/S. Make a small clear dash in pencil.

3. *Measure 1¼"(3cm) both sides of all these marks*. Draw lines across the complete square from these measured points - **don't rule a line from mark to mark** (see diagram). Continue measuring and ruling until you complete the grid. Rule lines on the R/S and draw them *very, very lightly*.

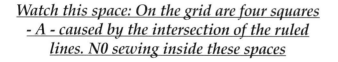

*Watch this space: On the grid are four squares - A - caused by the intersection of the ruled lines. N0 sewing inside these spaces*

### Start Stitching - *(Seam allowance not needed.)*

1. Fold the fabric on one set of marks and align the ruled grid (push a pin through from one side of the material to the other matching the lines). Sew across the grid starting and stopping at the cross junctions of the lines (edge of **A** squares) exactly as in the diagram overleaf (Fig.1). Repeat on the next set of marks. Two thick tucks have been created with **A** sections omitted in the stitching.

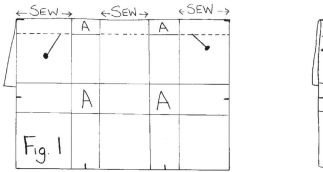

Fig. 1

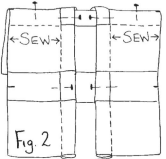

Fig. 2

2. Turn the piece round; fold the tucks to the centre. Pin in place. Fold the fabric on one set of marks as before, aligning the ruled lines. **Only stitch** from outer edge to the junction of previous stitching and drawn line at **A**; stitch from **A** to the outer edge on the other side (Fig. 2). Repeat this manoeuvre on the remaining set of marks.

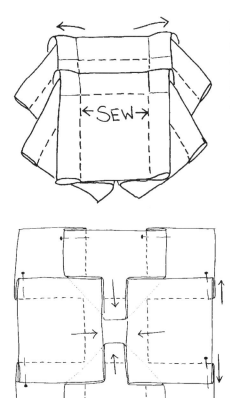

3. Turn the first set of tucks away from the centre - just have faith! Stitch the remaining parts of the lines between the junctions matching the ruled lines. It is now a really odd looking piece.

4. Lay flat. Turn the tucks towards each other - centre ones all face into middle - tucks on the edge turn towards the corners. Put pins on the outer edge to hold in place.

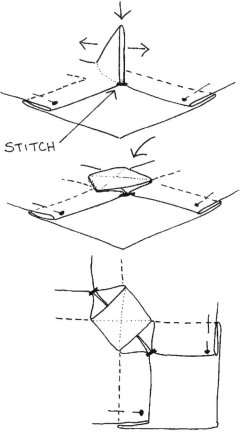

At these junctions you will find that it does not lie flat but forms a triangular shape. Lift the triangle up, and secure the base of the triangle (where the tucks touch) with a small stitch through all the layers. Now squash the triangular 'mountain'. This is really a case of pulling it outwards and flattening rather than a straight squash. Magically a square (on the diagonal) forms in the very centre. This is a variation on the Origami Twist (first featured in **'Tucks Textures & Pleats'**). Carefully press all pleats into place.

## Explore the Possibilities

For something that has such a curious title, there are lots of possibilities. You have pleats that you can play with, pockets to put things in and a middle you can twiddle. Experiment and see what you can do with it. Tuck a different piece of material under the tucks, filling in the corners and/or the centre. Stitch round the tucks to hold in place. Try a scrap of 'scrunched' or pin-tucked fabric under the centre folds. How about a really tiny 'Origami Twist' in one of the spaces?

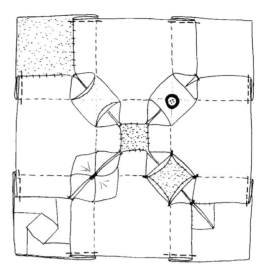

Tuck a folded square under the tucks - fold the square as shown in the diagram (Sharon Square), remove the small securing stitch and insert 'Sharon' under

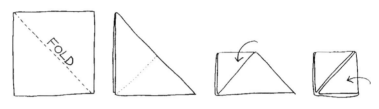

the tucks. Stitch edge of tucks( through all layers) to secure. 3"(8cm) squares were used in the photograph.

Secure the four corners of the Twist through all layers; roll the edges. How about inserting a different colour, then rolling the edges over it?

Bring two opposite sides of the Origami Twist together for a 3D effect. Hold with a bar tack or small stitch as shown below. Why not try turning each set of four pleats in the same direction (alternating one set clockwise and the other set anti/counter clockwise), catch the centre and add some Somerset or Sharkstooth patches?

***Finally, baste the tucks down to hold in place. Keep the basting inside the ¼"(0.5cm) seam allowance.***

*Why Sharon Square? A lady once asked me the name for this method of folding. I said that I didn't think it had one, and why not call it after her? Hence the Sharon Square came into being.*

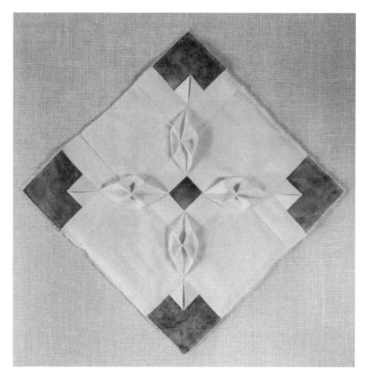

# Puffball Block

As ever, it is very hard to think of a name for these textural niceties. How else could you even begin to describe a square with padded, puffy pockets which are really stuffed tucks? There will be someone out there who will have an amazing name for this individual design. Why not write in with a suggestion? Polite ones only, please.

Life is curious thing. Here am I writing a book on 'Nipping and Tucking' having set out many years ago to be a doctor. Failing to achieve my ambition due to various family circumstances, I ended up in the 'Tea and Buns' business i.e. catering trade. Actually it was good fun. I did a management training course with a large company and had a whale of a time. They sent me to all kinds of places including Buckingham Palace. Yes indeed - I have had tea with the Queen! We did all the catering for the Garden Parties. I remember it well - the dappled sunshine, clink of teacups etc. In reality it was a mad bunfight with all these 'hoi polloi' stuffing as many scones, buns and sandwiches that they could possibly fit in their mouths, handbags and pockets, downing as much of the inferior champagne as was possible and shouting loudly to be heard above the din. Meanwhile Her Majesty sat in solemn seclusion in her special tent supping the finest tea from porcelain cups, gawped at by the milling multitude.

Talking about food and stuffing, did you know that the best fish and chips in the world are in New Zealand? Unlike the British chippies, they cook fresh chips for each customer in one or two portioned little baskets. The chips are pre-blanched then cooked. In my opinion this makes for a better chip; it is certainly much crisper. The fish in N.Z. is different - they have snapper, gropers and varieties that one can only guess at because of the pronunciation. Believe you me, there's nothing like a groper and chips on the beach at Mission Bay. I can really recommend the groper!!!

As I travel so much these days I have learnt not to be so suspicious of unusual foodstuffs and will try most things. There have been occasions when I have been a little surprised at what is put in front of me such as the deep fried onion rings that I ordered in Florida. I did not expect little sausages with creamy stuff in but Hey! it's America - they eat funny stuff there, like jam with everything! Obviously they have slightly different ideas about onion rings. Anyway the dish was duly consumed, cleared away and then my onion rings arrived. I could see out of the corner of my eye the staff having a natter about something and some customer demanding to know where his starter was. Silly waitress, she had given me the wrong food. I didn't realise anything was amiss. (Why should I? It's America. It's foreign!) No one ever queried it so I kept quiet and ate the onion rings as well! Psst - did you know they eat jelly with salad in the States!!!!! (As my favourite breakfast grub is anchovy paste and cucumber on toast I should not criticize.)

To be fair, I find the food in all countries including my own varies tremendously from the remarkably good to the appallingly awful. It pays to read the menu, ask questions and look particularly carefully at buffets. There was the dreadful occasion when inadvertently I poured custard over my salad thinking it was mayonnaise. This was an unusual combination to say the least, and not to be recommended!

# Puffball Block

(photograph on page 69)

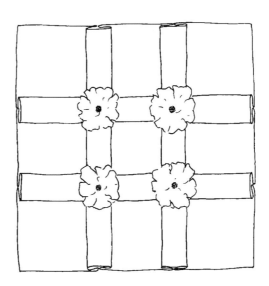

Like the Multiple Origami Twist, this is all one piece of material, but there are various places to slip in other colours and assorted bits to twiddle and fiddle. The inspiration came from a particular design titled 'Crossing over the Tucks' which was featured in both the last books. Once again this will seem to be very complex, but follow the diagrams carefully and it is really very simple - just complicated to describe. Have courage and give it whirl!

Minimum quantity of fabric required (sufficient for two): 18"(48cm) x 44"(115cm)

### Prepare the Pieces

1. Use the rotary cutter and ruler to cut the following square, or make a paper template (use newspaper); pin in place, draw round and cut out.

*To make the Puffball Block cut:* One 17½"(43.5cm) square
*(Same size as Multiple Origami Twist (page 63) - save time and cut two)*

2. Measure and mark exactly as described on page 63. All marks on the R/S; pencil lines in very lightly.

### Start Stitching - *(Seam allowances not needed.)*

Stitching technique is identical to the Multiple Origami Twist (page 63 -64) ***BUT all lines of stitching MUST stop ½"(1.25cm) from the A squares*** on all sides as shown below and overleaf (Fig. 1).

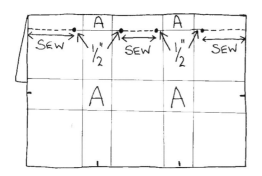

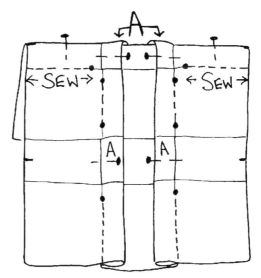

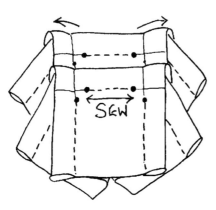

SEW

Fig. 1

3. Lay the piece flat on the ironing board. The tucks are going to be squashed flat and pressed. Use a fine slat, bias bar or a thin ruler to aid the squashing process. Insert bar/ruler into the tuck and press flat.

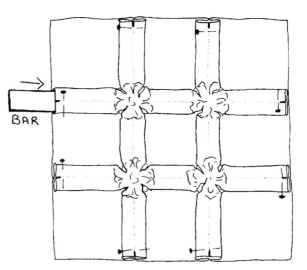

BAR

Try to keep the tucks squashed evenly over the seam line. Pin in place. There will be a puffy excess at the intersection of the tucks. Pencil lines may be removed with an rubber (UK) or an eraser (USA).

4. Turn the block over and lightly stuff these puffs through the small hole - use small pieces of torn polyester wadding/batting. To contain the stuffing pin a scrap of material (approximately 2½"(7cm) square) over the hole. Turn to the R/S and secure the scrap with a small stitch on the four corners as below.

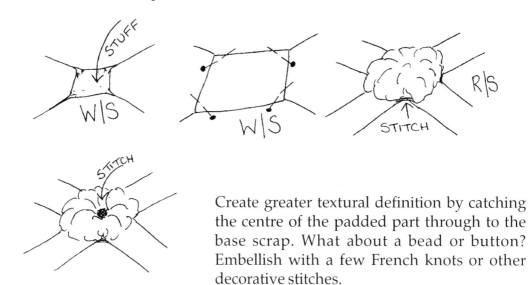

STUFF

W|S

W|S

STITCH

R|S

STITCH

Create greater textural definition by catching the centre of the padded part through to the base scrap. What about a bead or button? Embellish with a few French knots or other decorative stitches.

## Explore the Possibilities

Tuck a different piece of material under the tucks, filling in the corners and/or the centre. Stitch round the tucks to hold the material in place. Why not slip some tucked up, scrunched or finely pintucked textured fabric underneath?

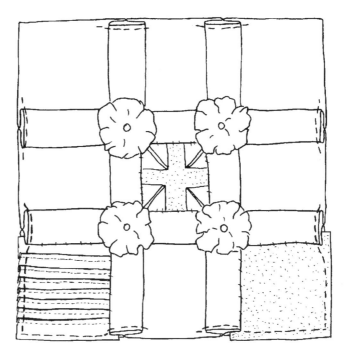

Make some 3"(8cm) Sharon Squares (see page 65) and insert it under the tucks. Stitch edge of tucks through all the layers to secure.

Finally baste down all the tucks round the raw outside edge to hold flat and in place. Keep the basting inside the ¼"(0.5cm) S/A.

# Folded Fabrication

Don't we make life hard for ourselves? Sometimes the simplest move turns into the most complex procedure imaginable. This seems to happen quite frequently when you decide to take short cuts. I think that 'Murphy's Law' often works overtime. How many times have you thought that it would be a really neat move if......? Only to discover that you have totally fouled things up and will have to start all over again.

I had never intended to have such a complicated life. At the tender age of eighteen all I wanted was to be a doctor, get married, have loads of children and that was it. Actually if I am really honest, I thought that I would live in sin rather than marry as it would shock my parents, but I had every intention of getting duly hitched up at some point. What happened? I went into 'Tea and Buns' (as previously mentioned), got married, worked for an airline, got pregnant, had the brat, got unmarried, ran a restaurant, got remarried and unmarried again, ran a village shop and a pub in between. Had several relationships, learnt patchwork, found latest man and wrote two books. Not quite what was intended. As my brat said on one never to be forgotten occasion - 'Mother, you are very talented in many ways but you are lousy at choosing your men!'

One leaps from crisis to crisis, and if I did everything properly half the time there would be no problem. The trouble is that I try to cheat. Mentioning the brat reminds me of the times when I promised that I would hand wash some special item of clothing and then forgot. The way round this is give the collar and cuffs a quick scrub, blot dry with a towel, hang on the line, and when he comes home gaily shout 'It's on the line but the collar and cuffs may be damp still!'. He believed it every time. (For really dirty marks scrub and blow dry with the hair dryer.) I remember the number of times I machine washed when specifically told to hand wash, then having to stand in front of the washing machine so that he could not spot the item going round. Usual way of tackling this was to send him out on some errand until the machine finished its cycle and you were safe.

# Folded Fabrication

This manipulation is a complete finished unit by itself needing no further work. Here it has been applied to a square of the background material. Of course, you could use the design on any other part of the quilt. It may be made any size but the dimensions given are suitable for appliquéing on to a 12½"(31cm) square.

Minimum quantity of fabric required for one block: 24"(60cm) x 44"(115cm)

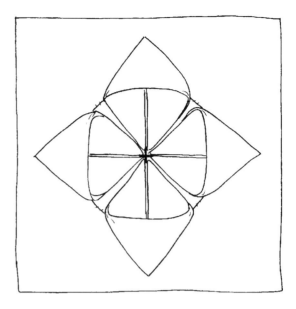

### Prepare the Pieces

1. Use the rotary cutter and ruler to cut the following squares or make paper templates (use newspaper). Pin in place, draw round and cut out.

*To make a Folded Fabrication cut:*

One 22½"(57cm) square

From the background material cut:

One 12½"(31cm) square

### Start Stitching - *S/A ¼"(0.5cm)*

(The first stages are identical to beginning Cathedral Window patchwork. No groaning - this method is done by machine.)

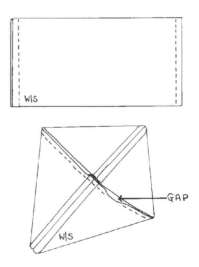

1. Fold in half R/S together, and using a ¼"(0.5cm) seam sew up the sides making a bag. Open and bring the sides to the middle, matching and opening seams. Sew along the raw edge; *leave a gap* and sew the remaining section.

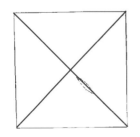

2. Cut the corners off; clip the centre seams; turn R/S out through the gap (bet you didn't leave a big enough one); close the hole with slip stitch but do not stitch into the underneath layer. (This is not totally necessary - only for pernickety people!)

3. Very carefully press the block, *taking great care not to stretch the edges* which are on the bias. Find the midpoint of all four sides (**ABCD**) by folding in half; gently press the crease; open out and repeat in the opposite direction. Mark all midpoints (on seamed side) with a small pencil dot or use a pin.

4. Lay the block with the seamed side *downwards*. Fold the sides to the centre so that they touch in the middle and the marks or pins at **A/C** align. (Seams will form a 'V' shape.) Press carefully. Pin across the centre as in diagram.

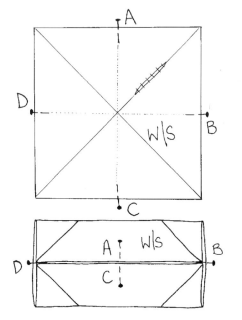

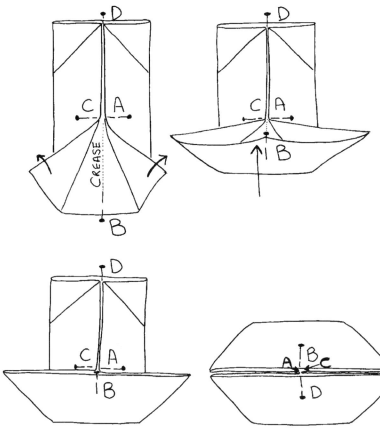

5. Open out the pleat by lifting the corners and bring **B** to the centre and to touch **A/C** (makes a boat shape). Pin in place. Repeat on the opposite side, and bring **D** to centre to touch **A/C**. Pin and press. All the folds will be aligned and you have formed a lozenge shape.

Give it a twiddle until this is so. Secure **ABCD** at the centre with a small cross-stitch through all the layers. *This will show so do it carefully*. A bead may be attached at the same time. Think about the colour of thread - try a contrast?

*Alternatively, it is possible to stitch at A/C initially and remove pins. Then turn the block, arrange the folds and stitch again across B/D.*

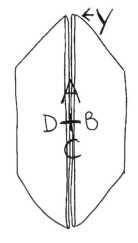

6. Lift one of the folded triangular corners up. The *tip* of the triangular corner is **Y**. *Open out* the folded triangle by pulling apart, and bring **Y** to meet **ABCD** at the middle; squash it flat and arrange. This shape will form a square section. Repeat with the three remaining triangular corners. Press gently to retain the creases.

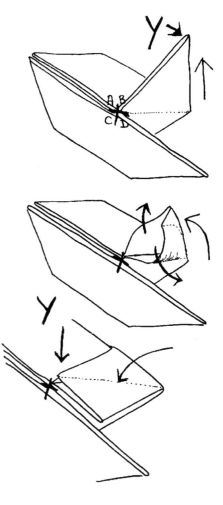

7. Lift **Y** up and pull outwards, back and away from the middle revealing the folds underneath (Fig. 1). This makes a petal-like shape, repeat with the remaining three corners. There are now four 'petals' (see photograph on page 70). If desired, lengthen these 'petals' by pulling **Y** further away from the centre. The final design depends on your creative inclinations. The shape is now complete. Attach it to the 12½"(31cm) background square by refolding the **Y** corners to form the square as described in stage 7. Decide whether you prefer the block placed diagonally, or parallel to the sides of the background material. Press the background square in half and half again either diagonally or straight across depending on the previous decision. Align the shape with the creases; pin carefully in place and apply by hand or machine to the fabric, through the *lower layer only* as Fig. 2.

Now pull the **Y** corners out and arrange to suit (see photograph on page 70). Stabilise the folds with a small stitch wherever needed to retain the textural form.

Fig. 1

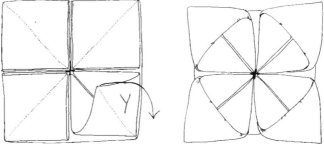

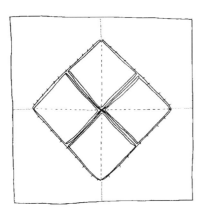

For additional interest the pleats and folds can be manipulated, the 'petals' shortened or lengthened, and/or contrasting fabric tucked into the layers. Change the original measurements of the initial square and make the block a different size, and apply to any part of the quilt. How about small ones for embellishing the corners? Try it for fun!

Fig. 2

# Fancy Fandango

One of the best fandangos I ever had was with a smashing guy who had an even more smashing car. He had a deep, dark brown growly voice, lovely eyes, was tall and handsome but just a smidgen bald on top. The car was purrfect; an enormous, low-slung, really speedy, open topped Jag. I gather it was the top of the range. Very impressive. If I wasn't going to fall in love with him I would definitely fall for his car.

He rang. We talked and then we met but not in some squatty pub or bistro - we went to the Ritz! He certainly knew how to win his women. This was the time to roll out the 'crown jewels', the really posh frock and rescue the moth-eaten mink. You do feel a bit of a pillock (idiot) traveling on the train in the late afternoon dressed in your evening finery, but it's by far the easiest way to get there. I always get lost in London, but the train driver should know the way to Waterloo. (To digress for a moment, my mother always worries about finding the way, and on one occasion whilst flying to New Zealand; brought her world atlas on to the plane in case the 'driver' needed any help. Can't you hear the conversation; 'The best way is to turn right at Bombay, follow your nose to Australia and go straight on at Sydney'.) Got to Waterloo, found a taxi and off to the Ritz. At this time I did not know what he looked like and I was totally prepared for the worst. I could imagine the 'phone call to my mother 'Right wally last night - had no teeth, no hair, was ninety if he was a day and what a bore!'. No, this one even looked OK. Tall, graying round the temples, aquiline features and a noble head of hair. We had a superb time and actually arranged to meet again. I went to several upmarket venues in London with him and he behaved pretty impeccably, to my chagrin.

At last the planned-for seduction scene arrived. We went to the theatre and afterwards out for a late supper. It became too late for my train and naturally he suggested that I stayed with him. We didn't go to a neat pad in Belgrave Square or some posh hotel but to his friend's flat in Outer Somewhere. Halfway through the inevitable wrigglings on the sofa, he fell asleep. Glory be - he snored like an asthmatic elephant! I stuck this patiently for a couple of hours ever hoping that my luck would be in. No chance.  Now I understand why his wife left him: to listen to that musical chorus night after night would try the patience of a saint. I snuck out quietly, although I do not know why I bothered as nothing would ever wake him up. Only one problem where was I? It was five in the morning and here I was lost in semi-suburban London. Total blind panic. All this being a 'liberated woman of town' nonsense left me and I was just a poor, little, lost person who just wanted to go home. Fortunately a street cleaner told me where to find the nearest Underground station and was somewhat surprised to be asked where we were. I suspect he was also a bit puzzled as to why I was fully dressed in a long gown and of course, wearing the 'crown jewels'. We never met again because he felt really peeved and put out that I had abandoned him - just as well, as I could not have lived with the snoring.

74

## Fancy Fandango

Make this any size, attach it anywhere and it's probably quicker to do it by hand! Use it for embellishing, decorating a plain border (see photographs) or appliquéd to the sashing. The design is constructed from folded layers of material forming a fairly thick sandwich which is stitched into place. This may render it too substantial for a sampler quilt block, but it has many other uses.

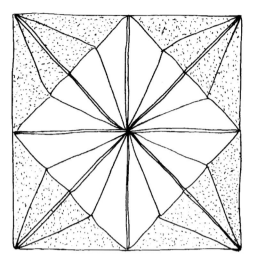

Should you wish to include these in the Quilt you must decide how large you want your finished FF to be: multiply this size by two and cut two squares to this measurement. The Fancy Fandango ends up half the size of the original square.

(Minimum quantity of fabric required for three x  3"(7.5cm) squares:)
(7"(18cm) x 44"(115cm)

### Prepare the Pieces

1. Use the rotary cutter and ruler to cut the following squares, or make a card template; lay on and draw round; cut out.

*To make a 3"(7.5cm) Fancy Fandango cut:*

Two 6"(15cm) squares - use two colours if desired

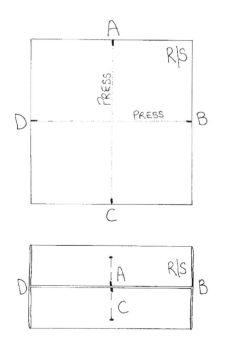

**Start Stitching** (S/A not applicable to construction.)

1. Select the first square - this will be the base (spotted in diagram) section. Press in half and in half again (not diagonally but into quarters) to find the centre. Fold two sides to the centre matching **A** and **C**; R/S on the outside. Press carefully. Pin on marks at centre. Make the lozenge shape as described on page 72 by following the folding instructions in stages 4 - 5. Either pin or stitch at the junctions. Press well. Complete the folding by following stage 6 (page 73) to form the square with all **Y** points to the centre as shown in diagram at top of next page. Press again.

75

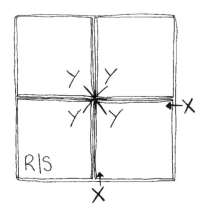

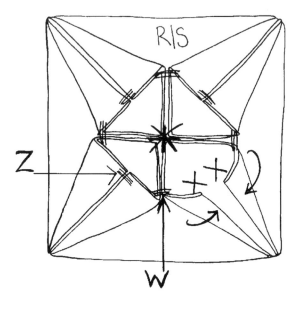

2. Stitch through all the **Y** points to secure all the layers. Take the opposite **folded** corners of one square at **X**, and fold inward.

Align both folded edges evenly and exactly with the diagonal of this square. *The folded edges are butted together*, not the raw ones. Secure the join at **Z** with a small hand stitch across the folded corners as shown above; sew through all the layers if desired*. Repeat with the remaining three sections. In addition, anchor the folds at **W**. Don't press at this stage as some of the 3D textural form may be lost.

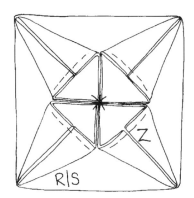

*The stitching may be through all but the last layer if preferred, then no sewing will show on the underside. That's this bit done. Really difficult wasn't it?*

3. To make the top section (unspotted in original drawing on previous page), take the remaining 6"(15cm) square. Repeat stages 1 - 2 as before, but extend stitching across **Z** and through **W** to hold the pleats firmly in place (shown in diagram above). For this part sew through all layers, as the back will not show.

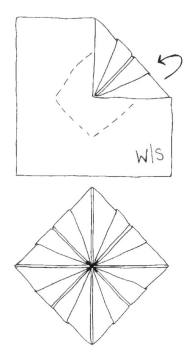

4. Using this *second textural shape*, turn over and bring the four corners to the centre. Secure all four points together and through all the layers with a nice *tidy* cross stitch (*will show*). *This is now the R/S*.

6. Lay the second square diagonally on to the first. It will touch the mid points of all sides on the first square. Pin in place. By hand, anchor the four corners of the second square to the under section before securing all the centre layers together. If preferred you could stitch right round all the outer edges of the second square to seal the join totally.

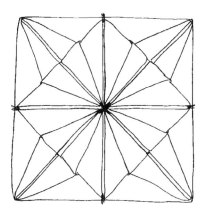

So far I have suggested stitching the entire piece by hand. This is the neatest way to achieve the final result. Stitching the design on the machine is equally easy and probably more robust, although the back of the block may not be so neat and tidy. If you have no objections to the appearance of the underside then try machining in this fashion:

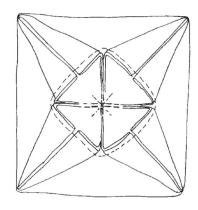

At stage 3 instead of using a cross stitch, pin carefully and run the machine back and forth over the four corners, using the normal presser foot. North - South first; then East - West. Raise the presser foot and bring the corner folds to the centre (as in stage 4), and sew round in a circle anchoring all the layers through **Z**. Much faster but the underside is not so attractive - does it matter? An even quicker method is to place the darning/hopper foot on the machine; go forwards and backwards at the centre; jump to the **Z** places and catch (running back and forth). Trim all threads.

### Be Creative with a Fancy Fandango

Embellish the centre with beads or French knots. Try a matching button.

Hang tassels on the corners.

A thought - make a further base (stages 1 - 2) from an additional 3"(7.5cm) square, place a completed FF on top and have a three-tiered Fancy Fandango! Embellish a box lid with it.

## Using the FF

Make three more. Stitch together and attach to a 12"(31cm) square of background fabric. Why not make just one giant FF? Use two 14"(36cm) squares then hand or machine appliqué as in drawing.

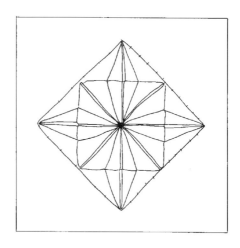

Construct a whole series in different colours and stitch together, as in photograph opposite page 51.

Use to embellish, conceal and titivate any badly seamed junctions. Of course this would never apply to you - you are using them purely for decoration!

Make a stiffened box by pinning and pressing the shape *only*, working through stage 1 (page 75) to the start of stage 2 on page 76. Open all the folds and insert a piece of cardboard and some wadding/batting. The card will need to measure a fraction less than the pressed square, or just under half the size of the square at the start: i.e. a finished 6"(15cm) square will take marginally less than a 3"(7.5cm) square section of board. Refold the creases, stitch down and continue to the end of stage 2. Make the additional second section and attach on top. Five stiffened Fancy Fandango sections plus one fabric covered and wadded piece of card for the bottom could be used for the box.

Make one FF in Christmas fabric, and to conceal any stitching attach an additional second section to the back. Hang it on the tree.

Finally, make a giant one and enclose a cushion/pillow pad. If you do this then I advise stitching round the entire outside of the second section to anchor it very firmly through to the base segment. Suggest that the enclosed pad be washable as you will not wish to unpick all the stitching each time just to launder the article.

'Fantasy in Fabric' (84" x 100") - textured blocks with Tucked Up Fan border, machine pieced & hand quilted. (Joan Ryan)

Tucked Up Fan cushion with Fancy Fandango box. (Jennie Rayment).

'Luscious Lilies' (27" x 27") - microwave dyed fabrics, machine pieced & quilted. (Jennie Rayment).

Corners on Log Cabin lap quilt (29" x 29") microwave dyed fabrics, machine pieced & quilted. (Jennie Rayment).

Sampler quilt (48" x 48") - microwave dyed fabrics. (Top row L-R ) Textured Star, Puffball Block, Eight Petal Flower, (Centre row L-R) Stuffed Squares, Driven dotty, Multiple Origami Twist, (Bottom row L-R) Folded Fabrication, Dutchmans Puzzle & Four Pointed Flower, Fancy Fandangoes on junctions, machine pieced & quilted. (Jennie Rayment).

# Driven Dotty

Idly perusing an old smocking book and an ancient origami manual one day, I was struck by a similarity between two forms of manipulation. So I fiddled and jiggled and guess what - twiddled - and here it is!

No one ever told me that teaching can drive you demented let alone dotty. I would suspect that I was probably potty to begin with, or maybe it's the creeping onset of senility that makes one behave a trifle eccentrically. For instance, to irritate the current man I wander down the street and every so often cock my leg over the tall metal bollards. It annoys him because I look stupid and he can't lift his leg so high. This is all very well providing you do not wear a petticoat. One day, I hoiked up leg, remembered to raise skirt but forgot the petticoat. The petticoat caught on the bollard, and there I was suspended from the post, stopped in my tracks and looking more ridiculous than normal.

This little incident reminds me of the psychiatrist who rang one day in response to one of my 'Seek Gent' letters. He picked a moment when I was not feeling terribly serious-minded, so his very pertinent questions were answered somewhat flippantly. He rabbited on and on so much about the need for relaxation and communication that I got seriously bored and very quietly climbed on the exercise bike. At least I would get the body worked out even if the mind had gone into zombylike oblivion. He was quite puzzled about the slightly heavier breathing and I think this gave him some strange ideas! Could I get rid of him? He must have phoned a dozen times purely for a chat. Obviously could not quite fathom out this odd lady mainly because I resorted to wildly exaggerated truths about my exploits, and the odd fib or two. We never met, and to this day I shall never know if he was tall, dark and handsome or short, squatty, spotty and bald.

After this one, I met an absolute menace who was hung up on football and religion. If he wasn't showing me the lumps on his feet caused by kicking the ball he was pressing biblical tracts into my hands and intoning phrases from the Good Book. I have no objection to any of this, but what really shocked me was the word he put on the Scrabble board. There we were innocently playing Scrabble - his go - and he put down a certain part of the male anatomy. Glory Be! What if the child came in and saw it? (He was all of 22 but I had to keep him pure!) So I did an 'Aunt Ann' to the board. Neat manoeuvre, first made by my aunt when she realised that she was losing - all you do is tip the board up 'accidentally on purpose', apologise profusely and abandon the game.

It nearly drives me completely round the bend trying to remember the name of the latest guy. There could be nothing worse than whispering 'John' in a moment of passion, if his name was Tony. I have always envied a friend of mine who has had two husbands and a current 'gentleman friend' and they all have the same name. Did she plan this or was it a happy accident? A further friend of mine has a plaque on her kitchen wall that states 'Love thy neighbour as yourself - but don't get caught.' Perhaps it should say 'Love thy neighbour as yourself (call them all Fred) - then you won't get caught!'

# Driven Dotty

Another block where you **_must_** follow the diagrams. It is not hard to construct but the *diagrams are very important*. Remember this is meant to be a workshop manual: sitting up in bed with bleary eyes reading the words is not the same as actually following the instructions stage by stage. Many of the techniques in this book are simple if you read the 'destructions' and systematically do them at the same time in the correct order. Should you not achieve the desired result - panic not; what you have constructed may be *much more better*!!!

Minimum quantity of fabric required for total block: 24"(60cm) x 44"(115cm)

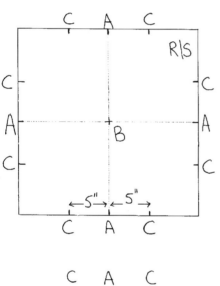

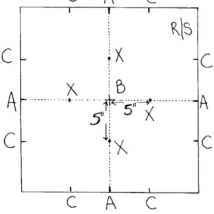

## Prepare the Pieces

1. Use the rotary cutter and ruler to cut the following square, or make a paper template (use newspaper for economy). Pin in place, draw round and cut out.

### *To make Driven Dotty cut:*
One 22½"(57cm) square
(This is same size as 'Folded Fabrication'. Why not cut out two squares together?)

2. Fold in half from side to side (*not diagonally*) and press; repeat on other side. On the R/S mark the mid point **A** of all four sides with a *small dash*. Mark the centre **B** with a *small dot* (**B** is at the junction of pressed creases). *Use a pencil.* Measure 5"(13cm) *either side of all A mid points* to find **C**; make another small mark.

### *All marks are on the R/S - be careful - make clear, small, tidy ones - blooming great splodges may be difficult to remove!*

3. Working from mid point **B** measure 5"(13cm) along all four pressed creases to find **X**; mark **X** with a *small dot* on R/S - north, south, east and west.

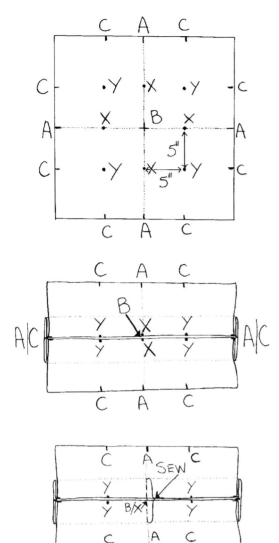

Complete the marking (on R/S) with four more dots at **Y** at 5"(13cm) intervals from **X** as in diagram. *There are now nine dots outlining a square.* Remember it's called 'Driven Dotty'! All nine (**X,Y,B**) are in line with the ones (**A,C**) on the outer edge. If desired identify the dots *lightly* in pencil, or attach a small sticky label.

**<u>Start Stitching</u>** (S/As not applicable for construction.)

1. Make two parallel pleats across the material by bringing **C** to **A** on either side (resembles box pleat); (**X** and **Y** align with **A**). Align these folds with the original pressed crease. Press the new folds carefully, checking that you have folded through all the relevant dots. Sew across the entire box pleat through the centre **B** as in diagram; sewing across the pleated portion only. This stitching will show: use matching thread; tie off the stitching at both ends or pull through to underside and knot. For an alternative method start by dropping the feed dogs, stitch on the spot, raise the feed dogs, stitch, finish in the same way.

2. Open the pleat and rearrange as shown below. All four **X** marks are now touching **B** (centre). Opposite pairs of **Y** marks are also touching each other. All the folds and creases and relevant dots should line up - fiddle with it until it does. Press folds in place. Stitch as before across the entire pleat through the centre, and tie off ends again. (*Dotted lines represent folds underneath.*)

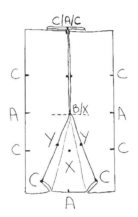

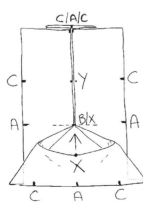

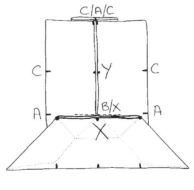

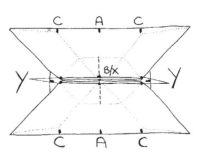

81

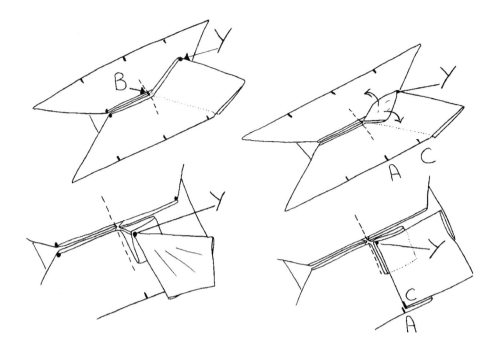

3. Take one of the corners at **Y**; open out; bring **Y** to the centre (**B**). Arrange the folds into a square. Pin in place. Repeat with the remaining three **Y** marks and it will resemble the drawing below. Wiggle the folds until everything is symmetrical. Press gently. Pin all the pleats especially those on the outer edges. All dots are aligned, and all folds lie straight and parallel.

4. Use a small stitch to secure the folds at **E** - 2½"(6.5cm) from the centre **B** (approximately). It is at the precise spot where both of the pleats underneath touch the square pleated corners on top. Look carefully then you will see it. Leave pins around the raw edge but remove the rest.

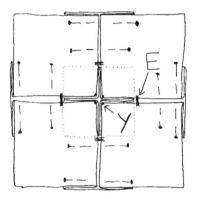

5. Now lift a folded corner up, hold 'Y' and pull back towards the corner of block. Repeat with the other three corners and there you are - a sort of folded flowery shape! Bet you didn't think that you could do it! This is now complete. Baste outer edges of the folds to prevent movement. Keep stitching within the usual ¼"(0.5cm) allowance or you may have to unpick at a later stage. P.S. Can't bear it when people refer to unpicking as 'reverse stitching' - they always say it so smugly!!

## Developments of the Design

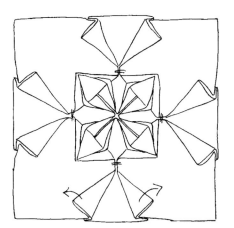

Fold the large pleats back. This will reduce the size of the block and you will have to add a border to adjust the size to 12½″(31cm) square.

Roll the edges and twiddle the bits. Use a small hand stitch to secure.

Tuck folded squares under the pleats.

Add beads or buttons for decoration.

Fold four 7″(18cm) squares in half diagonally. Lay one folded square on to each corner, aligning raw edges of square with raw sides of the block, and baste in place. Roll the folded edges back, and stitch to retain.

These squares could be made from two differently coloured triangles stitched together, then on rolling the edges another colour will show (see centre block of microwave dyed quilt opposite page 79)

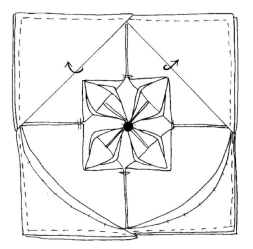

Just enjoy a good fiddle!

83

# More Ideas

The previous books contain lots of ideas which would make blocks for a sampler quilt. You will probably need one of them to be able to make the designs (see back page for ordering) as this chapter just deals with the specific measurements and brief instructions. Sadly there is insufficient space to give precise details, and anyway I have a deep objection to authors repeating themselves too often. There are at least fifteen more textured blocks to make, and this does not include any specifically twiddled variations that you may conjure up.

## From Tucks Textures & Pleats *(Page nos/photos refer to this unless specified.)*

**Tucked Panel** (Instructions on page 15 and photo opposite page 14 plus page 87 this book)

Cut strip 13½"(34cm) x 30"(75cm). Make ¼"(0.5cm) tucks. Trim to 12½"(31cm). Sew back and forth, twisting the tucks as you go. Experiment with different distances between the lines of stitching. Alternatively, make a large panel of tucks, cut this into small squares and arrange in different directions. Sew together, then twist tucks. Why not cut up tucked fabric into other shapes; piece together inserting bands of plain material? (See photograph on page 87 in this book)

**Woven Panel** (Instructions on page 31 and photograph opposite page 31)

Cut one 12½"(31cm) square in background material square + ten rectangles 12½"(31cm) x 4½"(11cm); cut these shapes with the longer length 12½"(31cm) across the width of material; experiment with a combination of colours. Press strips overlapping raw edges (pressed bands will measure approximately 2"(5cm) in width); insert padding if desired; stitch layers together. Weave. There will be a certain amount of space left around the woven portion - if preferred make an extra couple of padded bands or spread the pieces out. Don't forget you can always change the colour of the background material and let it show through the holes in the weaving. If necessary, catch the woven bands down through all layers to secure.

**Bias Bobble Panel** (Instructions on page 40 and photograph opposite page 31)

Cut one 12½"(31cm) square in background material square plus four 18"/19" (46cm/48cm) x 5"(13cm) bias cut strips. Use three diagonally across the centre, and cut the last one in half to fill the remaining space. Remember that you can embellish the tucked channels with stitch and/or insert a further colour, ribbon or lace.

**Trumpets** (Instructions on page 47 and photograph opposite page 30)

Cut eight 6¾"(17cm) squares. Construct as per instructions *but use ³/₈"(1cm) seam allowance*. The extra seam allowance makes it easier to position the second set of Trumpets. How about dual coloured Trumpets? Cut two 7¼"(19cm) square from two different colours and divide diagonally; piece together using ¼"(0.5cm) seams to form four dual coloured squares, and press seams open. Trim to 6¾"(17cm) square if necessary; fold into Prairie Points etc. Now you will have one colour on the inside and one colour on the outside! Add more interest by inserting folded squares.

**Triangle Cornet** (Instructions on page 52 and photo opposite page 53 and on front cover)

Cut four 7¼"(18.5cm) squares in background material. In addition cut four 6"(15cm) squares for the textured portions. Follow instructions for making up but *watch the centre junctions. Use ³/₈"(1cm) seam allowance*. For more detailed piecing explanation see Eight Petal Flower ('**Tucked Up in Bed**' - page 49 and 50 stages 3 - 5). Buttons are brilliant for covering little glitches!!

**Trumpet Voluntary** (Instructions on page 54 and photo opposite page 62 with six insertions)

Cut eight 6"(15cm) squares for the textured segments plus four 7¼"(18.5cm) squares in background material. Make the textured pieces - keep the basting within a ¼"(0.5cm) seam. Follow Eight Petal Flower ('**Tucked Up in Bed**' - page 49 and 50 stages 3 - 5) for piecing instructions. *Place the sections 1"(2.5cm) in from the raw edges not ³/₈"(1cm) as in text. Use ³/₈"(1cm) seam allowance*. Open the shapes, and Murphy's Law permitting they should touch, but you can always add a few beads or the good old covered button! (Block featured on calico quilt opposite page 20 in this book.)

**Origami Twist** (Instructions on page 69 and photograph opposite page 14)

Cut one 18"(46cm) square (extra fabric allowed for variations in size of manipulation). Pin 2½"(7cm) pleats and make the twist. Baste the pleats to secure, and trim to 12½"(31cm) square. Why not insert another colour in the centre and roll the edges of the Twist? Perhaps insert folded squares underneath the centre shape? If you prefer cut an even bigger square to begin with, make the Twist and play with the pleats; roll and stuff if you fancy! Trim the block back afterwards.

Experiment with a smaller centre (pin smaller pleats). Press pleats in place; turn the centre back in opposite direction and roll edges; flex the pleats. (Block featured on calico quilt opposite page 20 in this book.)

Use the same method of pleating to make a hexagonal Twist. Cut one 20"(50cm) hexagon; pin a 1¾"(4.5cm) pleat on each of the six sides. Carefully rotate all the pleats in the same direction as before - this needs extra twiddling to make all the folds lie flat. Yet again you can roll the centre and pad the pleats etc. Add extra borders to make up to 12½"(31cm) square. (Block featured on calico quilt opposite page 20 in this book.)

**Bow Tie** (Instructions on page 74 and photograph page 79)

Cut four 6½"(16cm) squares in background material plus one 8½"(22cm) square for the centre. Construct as per instructions and add four folded squares to the corners then roll the edges back as described in the method on page 83 in this book. The Bow Tie can be fairly boring, but there's no reason why you can't use the technique to embellish other places such as the junctions in the sashing as pictured on calico quilt opposite page 20.

## From Tucks & Textures Two *(Page nos/photos refer to this unless specified.)*

**Corners on Log Cabin** (Instructions on page 21 and photograph on page 20)

Use the same measurements as in the text but think about using a selection of colours both for the strips and for the squares. Continue with the technique until the block measures 12½"(31cm) square (keep going for five rounds of 'Log Cabin' up to and including the 5"(13.5cm) squares. *Watch your seam allowances - keep to ¼"(0.5cm).* A border can always be added to correct any little anomalies! Technique used in several of the quilts featured in this book.

**Contrariwise Cathedral Windows** (Instructions on page 28 and photograph on front cover & page 87 this book)

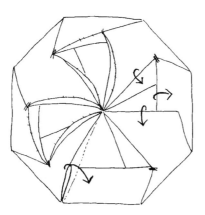

Cut one 22"(50/51cm) square for design plus one 12½"(31cm) of background material. Use the same construction technique as in the book. Cogitate (sounds awful!) upon the effect of tucking small folded squares into the rolled edges, or make a smaller Cathedral Window Square to insert under the central section - use a 6"(15cm) square. Roll open the folds of this insertion. Try twiddling the pleats in a different way as shown in diagram and on front cover ('**T & T 2**') .

### Interlocking Textured Shapes

**Squares**: (Instructions on page 12 and photographs on page 19 & opposite page 62).  Cut sixteen 6½"(16cm) squares. Experiment with colour and the direction that the shapes are rotated (see this book - Borders on page 92 for more information).

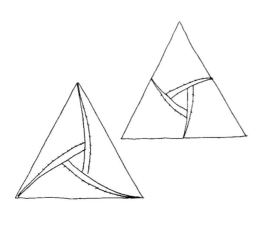

**Triangles**: (Instructions on page 14 and photograph opposite page 25 & page 87 this book). Cut eighteen 6"(15cm) equilateral triangles - 6"(15cm) being the length of the sides *not the height*. Again you could experiment with colours, rotation and which side you use. The triangles when interlocked form two quite different shapes - one side has three triangle sections and the other has three 'kite' shaped segments. As it is completely reversible you may choose which side to use.

**Hexagons**: (Instructions on page 15 and photograph opposite page 38 & back cover). Cut twenty-four 6"(15cm) hexagons to make the panel featured on the back of book. Construct the design and appliqué to one 12½"(31cm) background square. Why not cut six 12"(30cm) hexagons and try the padded and stuffed effect as detailed on page 17 ('**Tucks & Textures Two**') and shown on the calico quilt opposite page 20 in this book.

**Crossing over the Tucks** (Instructions on page 43 '**T & T 2**' and in  photograph below)

Cut one 20"(50cm) square. Make 1"(2.5cm) tucks. This block may need a fraction trimming off. Don't forget that you can tuck other colours under the tucks or insert textural pieces, twiddle the middles and/or play with the pleats.

**Triangle Cornet/Star Flower** (Instructions on page 46 '**T & T 2**' and in photo below)

Cut four 7¼"(18.5cm) squares in background material. In addition cut eight 4¾"(12cm) squares for the textured portions - *no need to cut out on the bias* as in the book: the design works just as well with straight cut shapes. On completion the Star Flower sections will almost touch the edge of the block - take care if trimming. On the calico quilt (photograph opposite page 20 - this book), the Star Flower inserts were deliberately cut larger {from 6"(15cm) squares} so that they would flood off the block on to the next design.

**Tucked Panel, Crossing over the Tucks, Interlocked Triangles, Contrariwise Cathedral Window and Star Flower (from top left clockwise)**

# Borders

How many times have you been to an art exhibition and exclaimed over a picture but agonized over the frame? Sometimes this is over dressy and swamps the picture or the selection of a plain unadorned edging makes an uninspiring painting even more so. You have just designed a picture, and whether it is large or small it will need a frame or border to complement the design. Adding a border will complete and add the finishing touch, increase the size and introduce more area for embellishment. There is no reason why you couldn't have several borders of differing sizes and patterns for a really elaborate appearance.

## Several Ways to Add a Border

**1.** Log Cabin - work systematically round the edges attaching the strips as you go. This technique produces unbalanced seams that I find unattractive.
**2.** Described in '**Tucks & Textures Two**' (page 23) has seams that pinwheel round the quilt. More attractive in my opinion but not quite so easy.
**3.** Mitred corners - not terribly easy for beginners.
**4.** Probably the easiest way - a border added to either side first then to the top and bottom.
**5.** Attached with corner squares in the same manner as sashing bands (page 97).

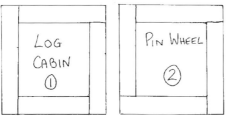 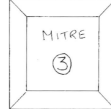 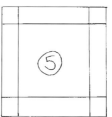

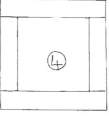

*<u>Whichever method you choose - you MUST measure carefully not once but twice before cutting.</u>*

## Tips for the Fourth Method

To keep the quilt square - measure the opposite sides; cut the borders exactly equal in length and make the quilt fit the strip. Pin carefully in several places. Measure the remaining sides and repeat. It's no good taking a long strip and gaily stitching it on, as inadvertently a little more will be added to one edge than the other and this causes distortion. *Have both sets of opposite sides the same measurement to keep the Quilt square and check that the <u>diagonal</u> measurements match, too.*

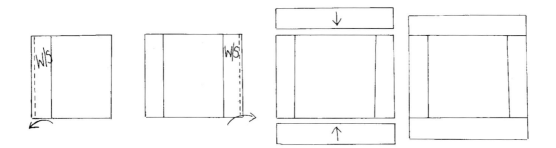

Decide on width of border, and cut the strips from **across** (*selvedge to selvedge - weft*) the fabric **not** down (*parallel to the selvedge - warp*) the material. In my opinion the only time you should ever cut down the cloth is when using a directional design. (See page 19 for more information.) Join if necessary, reducing the stitch length for a tighter and less visible link: sew together, open the seam and press flat. Don't attempt to match seams on opposing sides: slightly mismatched sets of seams are far more disturbing than randomly scattered ones, in my opinion.

## Interesting Borders

Why not have a textured or embellished border? You could intersperse fancy frames with plain ones, or add interest to the corners with a different design. Be absolutely OTT or intriguingly simple. Some of the following textural designs are featured in the previous books 'Tucks Textures & Pleats' and 'Tucks & Textures Two'. To avoid repetition, here are some brief instructions. These measurements can be changed to suit your quilt - the figures are as guidelines only.

### Appliquéd Borders

There are hundreds of different designs that could be applied to the border strips, and some of them lend themselves to trapunto (stuffing). Why not create a little interest by constructing bias strips (see page 28) and using a Celtic style of appliqué, either traced from an existing pattern or draw your own? An easy way of making any design fit a certain space is to cut some paper the exact length and width of the designated space; concertina the paper into as many portions as desired, and draw the design on the outside edge.

Now trace the design onto all the other sections - really boring. Try removing the thread from the sewing machine needle and carefully stitching round the lines. Hey Presto! All the lines are pricked through all the layers - one instant complete pattern.

**'Bias Bobble' Band** - (Featured in both books)
Finished border width **3"(8cm)**.

Measure length required. Cut a 3½"(9cm) wide strip of backing material on the straight grain to this length, plus two 2½"(6.5cm) wide bias strips to the same measurement. Find centre of straight grain strip by folding in half widthways (along the longer dimension), and press gently - lay flat when finished. Press under one edge of both bias strips by ¾"(2cm) and place on to the straight cut strip, butting the folded pressed edges to the central ironed crease. Pin well through all the layers, and sew a ½"(1.25cm) seam either side of the central folds - this will form two small tucks. Open out the tucks and embellish the channel with a decorative stitch, ribbon, lace, broderie anglaise or ric-rac braid. Close the tucks over the central embellishment and divide into sections (minimum length 2"(5cm), or more for preference), securing each with a small stitch. Leave ½"(1cm) either end to allow for the seams. Roll back the tucks to reveal the decoration (Fig. 1 overleaf), and sew the edges of the tucks down by hand or machine, or use the blind hem stitch (see page 29 of this book ).

Fig. 1

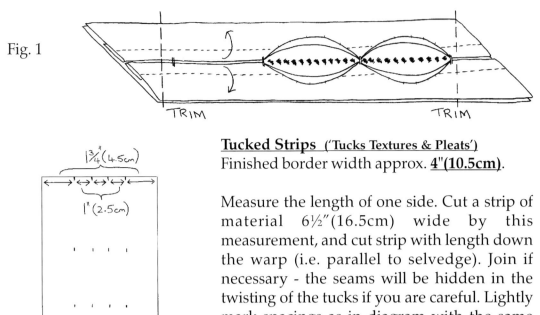

TRIM                    TRIM

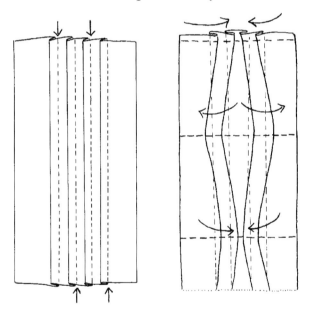

1¾"(4.5cm)

1"(2.5cm)

**Tucked Strips** ('Tucks Textures & Pleats')
Finished border width approx. **4"(10.5cm)**.

Measure the length of one side. Cut a strip of material 6½"(16.5cm) wide by this measurement, and cut strip with length down the warp (i.e. parallel to selvedge). Join if necessary - the seams will be hidden in the twisting of the tucks if you are careful. Lightly mark spacings as in diagram with the same spacings top and bottom and at intervals along the length.

Make four tucks by folding the material exactly on all marks (mark on edge of fold); sew ¼"(0.75cm) seam parallel to the fold. For the greatest accuracy press each tuck before you stitch. (Try to sew up and down the tucks alternately to prevent distortion.) Press all the tucks flat in one direction: press both R/S and W/S. Don't worry if the tucked seams on the W/S appear slightly uneven - once the tucks have been twisted this doesn't show! Repeat for any other sides.

Measure and mark tucked band at approx. 3"(8cm) intervals down the tucked section, or adjust the measurement to fit the relevant length of quilt.

On the first set of measurements, sew over the tucks turning the first pair of tucks towards the other two (the centre ones may touch). On the second set of measurements reverse the procedure - the tucks turn away from each other. Continue in this way until the entire line of tucks is twisted. Attach the tucked strips to the quilt as usual, i.e. place R/Ss together. Stitch and open out.

Experiment with designs by changing the spacing as you flex the tucks (thick tucks may distort if the spacing is too close), or sew a deliberately wiggly line for a curved effect. Explore the use of a decorative stitch to anchor the tucks, and/or attach ribbon or threads. Embellish the spaces between the tucks with ribbon or stitch. Any amount of tucks may be done and twisted in any particular pattern.

Have a play - you can't go wrong really and if you do does it matter? After all you did design it that way!!

### Trumpet Border ('Tucks Textures & Pleats')

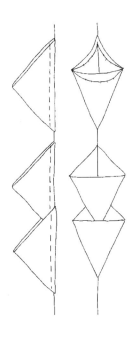

Trumpets are basically 'Prairie Points' which have been inserted into a seam then squashed, twiddled, fiddled and/or stuffed in many ways. Include them in any seam, make any size, then manipulate deviously.

To make one trumpet cut a square (any size) of material, and fold as on page 26 stage 2 (R/S on outside) to form a quarter triangle. Before inserting into a seam, baste the raw edges, using a really long stitch length on machine. Start at the end with two folds; check that the folds are aligned exactly then sew to the other end. Keep all basting within the ¼"(0.5cm) seam allowance. The trumpets can be laid down any seam either singly or tucked into each other. Baste in position on one edge before laying the other piece of material on top and completing the seam.

Once inserted into the seam there many different ways to manipulate this shape (see page 30 for some ideas). You could flatten the trumpet; secure at the corners; pad with small pieces of batting. Experiment with rolling the edges, inserting another folded square in a contrasting colour. Cover the seam with a further piece of material, tucking the raw edges under the rolled folds. Why not pull the shape off centre and roll edges to resemble a lily? You can even pleat one side and pad or make a small dart in the 'Trumpet' and then squash - two diddy shapes for the price of one.

### Double Squashed Box Pleat Tucks

Finished border width **3"(8cm)**

Measure length required. Cut 9"(23cm) wide strip of material by this measurement. Fold in half lengthways and gently press; lightly pin fold to secure. Rule line 1"(2.5cm) from folded edge. Rule second line 1¾"(4.5cm) from the first one. Sew both drawn lines. This is really, really hard! Press folds flat. Easiest method is to flatten the first seam, insert a standard school ruler (borrow the children's) into the second seam; wriggle the tuck evenly and press. That's it!

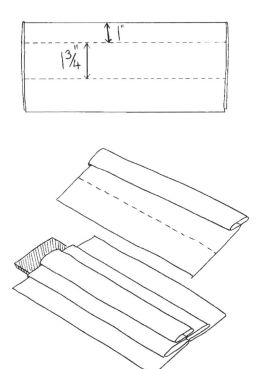

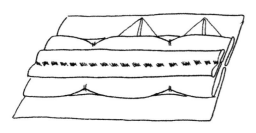

a. The double tucks can be rolled and caught in relevant places.

b. Embellish the central tuck with decorative stitch and/or ribbon, lace, threads etc.

c. Tuck one or two folded squares under the tucks. Stitch in place.

**Finally**, one last idea for a long border of the same design is the 'Crossing over the Tucks' technique from **'Tucks and Textures Two'** page 45.

## More Ideas for Borders

The border does not have to be made from one long continuous pattern. It could be constructed from individual sections stitched together to make the correct length. These sections could be squares, rectangles or any other combination of geometric shapes which preferably form a straight line.

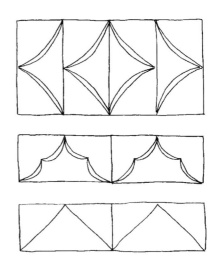

1. Why not use the block from the **Dutchman's Puzzle**? Try it horizontally or vertically with fancily twiddled edges or just plain.

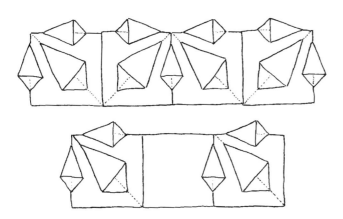

2. What about making the flower unit from **Luscious Lilies**? Intersperse the blocks with plain squares or rectangles. Link two blocks together, both sharing the central floret. The flowers can 'flood' off the strip on to a further plain border.

3. **Interlocking Squares** from '**Tucks & Textures Two**' creates an interesting border. Experiment with the direction of rotation of the design either clockwise or anti/counterclockwise. Try tucking another colour under the pleats (see photograph opposite page 51) .

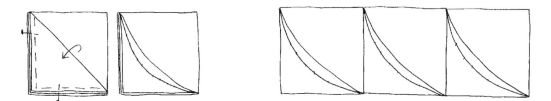

4. Take two squares of fabric; fold one in half diagonally and place on to the other, aligning all the edges. Pin and baste in place; roll the folded edge, stitch to secure.

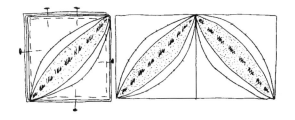

5. Take three squares; fold two diagonally; place on to the third square, butting up to each other. Pin, baste and roll the edges. Why not have the base square a different colour, or embellish the gap?

6. Contemplate using some of the folded shapes from all three books either diagonally in squares or in between the seams of the sections. Try a row of single Eight Petal Flowers or a line of florets from the Four-Pointed Flower or anything else you fancy.

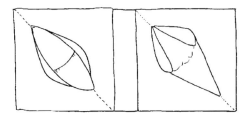

*Finally, why not mix and match some textured sections with plain strips inserted in between as in the drawing?*

<u>*BUT*</u> - the drawback to this kind of edging is the **Mathematics!**

Constructing from single units is completely different to making one long line - you may well be involved with major calculations. (Oh - to get involved with Major Calculations!! Wonder what he's like?) The very mention of 'hard sums' throws some people entirely, but *don't worry overmuch as you can always 'fudge' it and adjust any shortfalls with an extra piece or cut a bit off!*

To calculate the number or the size of any individual units *measure the length of the side to be bordered and deduct the seam allowances from this measurement.* Find a factor that is divisible into the required length - whether it's an odd or an even number of whole portions may not matter. Some designs are more attractive in pairs (even number of units), some look best if there is a central focus to the pattern (odd number of units).

For example (given in imperial measurements - same principle applies to metric):
edge to be bordered = 48½" minus S/As = 48"

This number can be divided in several ways - 8 x 6: 6 x 8: 12 x 4: 4 x 12: 3 x 16: 16 x 3: Therefore one could make a 3" border design constructed from sixteen 3" square units or a 4" border from twelve 4" units etc.

If the desired border design cannot be made to fit the available space then solve the problem by enlarging the quilt with an extra border to make the length mathematically viable. Naturally, this action upsets the mathematical proportions of the other sides so I suggest that you go and have a large drink or a cup of tea.

The mathematics of quilt making are nowhere as near as complicated as proving Kepler's Orange Stacking Theory. He wanted to prove mathematically that the best way to stack oranges is in rows with the next row balanced on the dimples in between. It took 250 pages of logic and 3 gigabytes of computer storage space to prove the theory. Can't think why he didn't ask the greengrocer!

## Creative Corners

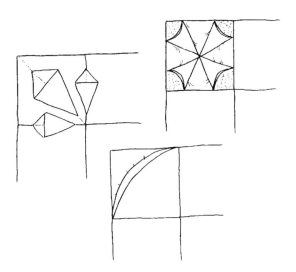

By attaching the borders in the same manner as the sashing bands (page 97) extra textural titillation can be added at the corners. Several of the designs from the block patterns or from the examples given in the previous section are suitable for embellished corners. Any design that is constructed in a square format may be used.

When calculating the size of square to use *don't forget to add on the seam allowances - probably ¼" (imperial): 0.5cm (metric)*. If the square is divided in any way then the seam allowances will alter.

## S/As for Divided Squares

A - Basic square - **add ½"(1cm)** to desired finished size.
B - Divided diagonally once - add ⁷/₈"**(1.75cm)** to desired finished size.
C - Divided diagonally twice - add **1¼"(2.5cm)** to desired finished size.

'Black & White' (60" x 60") - textured blocks with jet beads & button embellishment, machine pieced & hand quilted. (Jean Collett).

Wallhanging (32" x 44") - Tucked Up Fans, Luscious Lilies, Trumpets, Eight Petal Flower & Contrariwise Cathedral Window, machine pieced & hand quilted. (Peggy Douglas).

Lap Quilt (unfinished) with patchwork border to be added. (Joan Douglas).

'Memories of N.Z.' (39" x 62") - features all the blocks from 'Tucked Up in Bed', although some of the designs are different sizes. All the fabrics (apart from the border) were given by the New Zealand store owners that I visited. I asked each one to contribute a piece of material that typified N.Z. in their opinion and this is what I received! Every fabric has been used somewhere. There was no planning, the final design was pure happenstance. Machine pieced & quilted. (Jennie Rayment).

# Finishing Off

Let's turn all those assorted pieces into a sampler quilt; alternatively they could be stitched together and used as a throw, coverlet, tablecloth or duvet cover (either with or without any backing material). A quilt is a textile 'sandwich' created from two layers of material enclosing some form of interlining such as wadding/batting. The three pieces are usually anchored together with stitching, but there is nothing to stop one from stapling, pinning or even tying the layers with wire. (I would not suggest using these alternatives on the bed unless you like feeling scratchy!)

There are two ways to assemble a sampler quilt. The first method involves quilting the sections individually before finally constructing. Each block is usually sashed prior to the quilting. This manoeuvre may limit the design potential, especially if the sashing has been attached in a particular colour or pattern sequence; consequently you can't swap the arrangement of blocks so easily, nor can you be very inventive with the sashing desgns. In addition, accuracy is paramount with this system, once the block has been quilted it looses its 'jigglability' and cannot be pulled, pushed or stretched to fit all the others.

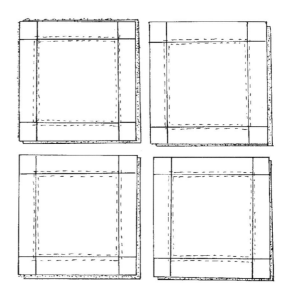

Furthermore, the quilt can be tricky to assemble by machine. It is possible to machine the blocks together but through the top layers only: the raw edges of the backing fabric need to be turned under and hand stitched together. This may cause a certain weakness to the structure as the interlining and backing fabric are in several pieces. Finally it is difficult to extend the outer edges of the quilt because you would have to add more strips of both backing material and interlining. On the other hand the quilting is easier as you can pop an individual block in a bag and complete it while waiting for the latest gent to turn up!

I prefer the second method which involves stitching all the blocks, sashing and borders together first, then layering the entire quilt with the wadding/batting and backing material, quilt and bind it as a whole. There are more possibilities with this technique for inventive arranging of the blocks, imaginative sashing and quilting designs which can flow freely across the entire creation. The wadding/batting and backing material are in one piece and the dimensions of the top section can be changed easily by adding or subtracting strips where required. The biggest problem is the somewhat daunting task of quilting the entire lot all at once. Do you have to quilt it all? Why not tie or secure the layers with buttons perhaps? (See Quilting page 101).

# Arranging the Design

Here you are surrounded with all those completed squares. What are you going to do? The first thing is to lay them all out somewhere and look at them. Aaah, don't they look nice sitting on the carpet! Somehow or other these unconnected blocks have to be assembled as a cohesive unit. It is the sashing that will bind all the blocks together and give the quilt some uniformity.

Lay out all the squares on the floor or anywhere you can really spread them out. Select one square for the centre (only possible if you have made 9, 15, 25 or 35 blocks). Place the other blocks in some form of order. I like to balance the design if possible. For instance the starry-like textured blocks (Four-Pointed Flower, Textured Star) could be opposite each other on either side as could the Multiple Origami Twist and Puffball. Balance the Stuffed Squares with the Dutchman's Puzzle. Tucked Up Fans are ideally suited for a corner as are Luscious Lilies.

As a general rule of thumb, I try to harmonise the colours and texture, i.e. don't have all highly textured ones in a solid row; insert a less heavily twiddled block in between. The same rule applies to the intensity of the colours. Try to view the proposed quilt from above. I don't mean break your neck falling off a chair, but lay the quilt out in the hall and go upstairs. As an alternative, try pinning the designs on to a large board and prop it up, or attach to a sheet and hang - use the washing line. Screw your eyes up to get an overview of the design. You may be fortunate to have one of the reducing lenses or why not buy a security viewer (usually fitted into a door). I just take my glasses off and it's all a pleasing blur!

Sometimes blocks do not fit into the network - they are too colourful, too boring, too over textured or you just don't like them. When this happens you could make another or replace it with a plain square that could be embroidered or quilted (see photograph page 50). Perish the thought, but some of the blocks may be have to be discarded because they are *not 12½"(31cm) square* - but why not *add a border to increase the size or trim off any excess*? Left over blocks could always be used for cushions/pillows, bags or table-mats or turned into shepherds pie.

The harmony and coordination of the entire piece will be greatly improved when the sashing is added. Add extra interest by texturing these bands (see Borders chapter). You could be more adventurous and experiment with a completely different layout of the pieces (see Playing with Layout page 98) or just stitch the whole jolly lot as one.

Once the layout is resolved, decide on the width of the sashing. This measurement will likely depend on the required size of the completed quilt. 3"(8cm) wide bands were used in all the examples (pages 9 - 11): *remember it's exclusive of S/As.*

## Adding the Sashing Bands

There are various methods of assembling sampler quilts. In my opinion the simplest and most accurate system is to sash round each block individually, attaching the strips and corner squares (as in description below) to the relevant sides, then stitching together. This technique makes it much easier to line up the seams of all the blocks.

As the sashing is linked with squares, why not take the opportunity to add an extra dimension to the design? Think about making these squares from different colours, or utilise the space for a pertinent quilting design. Create the squares from some form of texture such as a Trumpet (see lower diagram) or attach a Fancy Fandango (page 75). Be a little adventurous and explore the possibilities.

### Making the Bands & Stitching Together

1. Before you start any sewing either make a sketch of the layout or number in some way (use pinned or sticky labels), and indicate which way up the block fits in the design. There is nothing worse than discovering you have pieced one vital bit in the wrong place. Unpicking is a chore!

2. Lay out the quilt and count the number of sashing pieces and squares required. Cut out all the sections - use a rotary cutter if possible, or make a card template and draw round. The easiest method is to cut strips of the correct width and divide into the relevant lengths - *all lengths will be 12½"(31cm). Cut any strips across the material - from selvedge to selvedge*. (See Important Information section - Cutting Fabric on page 18.)

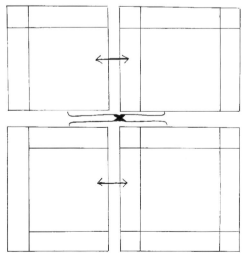

3. Stitch the sashing bands on to the sampler blocks as shown in the diagrams. Attach one piece of sashing to the block first; one square to the next sashing piece - stitch this to the block; repeat on the next side, and finally add a square to each end of the last strip and attach.

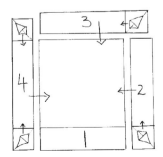

Press all the seams open and flat where possible. Work systematically, constantly checking that you have added the correct piece to the relevant side. One block alone will have sashing bands on all four sides, the others will have only two or three sections attached.

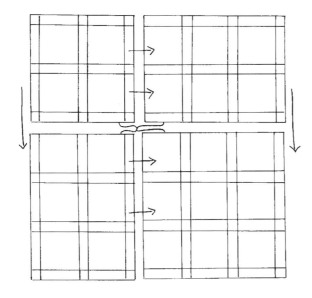

4. Join these enlarged squares together. Stitch two blocks to form a rectangle; repeat with two more; stitch the rectangles to make a larger square. Continue in this way until all the blocks are joined in bigger units of 4, 6 or 9 blocks. Now sew these together. Press seams open and flat. Quilt assembling should be easy, and using this technique is both simple and effective. Piecing the blocks in this fashion has the advantage of keeping the weight of the sections fairly evenly balanced - less likely to stretch when stitching.

There is a vogue for assembling sampler quilts by stitching all the blocks and sashing into long strips then stitching the strips together. As the quilt is built up it becomes heavier, and trying to attach a long, thin, light-weight strip to a large, heavy, fat portion sometimes causes 'drag' (stretching) and becomes very unwieldy.

5. Increase the size of the quilt to the desired measurements by adding more borders. Finally, press the quilt well. Reduce bulk by opening as many seams as possible.

## Playing with the Layout

Do you have to have sashing between all the blocks? Why not try something different? In the photograph opposite page 20 the centre section is composed of nine blocks sewn together without any sashing, then bordered. Go on - ponder over the pieces - attempt an alternative arrangement - be daring. The only fly in the ointment is the mathematics involved with fitting everything together.

**Always do all calculations based on the finished sizes i.e. without seam allowances; THEN add the seam allowances.**

It is very easy to get confused with the mathematics and miscalculate the mesurements of the next section. Scale drawings on graph paper are the proper remedy; sadly the very prospect terrifies most of us.

Who says that all the bands have to be the same width? Adjust the size of the connecting strips to fit the available space. Take care to be consistent and double check the mathematics before cutting anything. In a 'senior' (USA term) moment one day, I convinced myself that 8 x ½" = 2" not 4", and nothing would fit.

Try some new layouts - remember to do all the calculations exclusive of seam allowances. If you find that you have miscalculated - fret ye not - the borders can always be adjusted and you can add a little extra if needed. An extra boarder or two is always appreciated especially under the covers!!! (Sorry - couldn't resist it.)

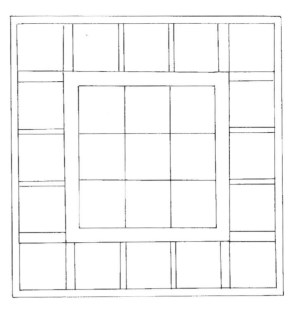

## Preparing for Quilting

As previously explained, a quilt is a textile 'sandwich' composed of three layers - top, wadding/batting and backing fabric. Purchase sufficient backing material and wadding/batting for the complete quilt top - err on the generous side. In my opinion, a thin, lightweight, low-loft (amount of puffiness) *washable* wadding/batting is best. (In Britain, 2 oz weight wadding is the norm.) Nowadays there are many kinds of batting available - select which one you prefer or ask advice from the shop. Ideally the backing fabric should be cotton, but there are some very good polyester and cotton mixes around that are suitable. Alternatively use an old sheet or purchase a new one.

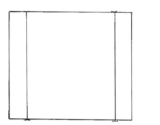

1. Join the backing material if necessary pressing all seams open. Wash the backing material - it is a large piece of cloth and if shrinkage occurs at a later date the result could be disastrous. Laundering also removes the dressing thus rendering it easier to sew through.

2. These layers have to be tacked/basted, pinned or tagged together before quilting. There are lots of different methods to achieve this. Many people have their own favourite technique. Personally I fall into the tacking brigade but can be persuaded to use the tagging gun. I prepare my quilts in the following manner:

3. Lay the backing material on the floor, firmly pull fabric flat and taut. Pin well to the carpet placing pins at 45°. Lay the wadding/batting down, retain by hooking over the pins. Carefully lower the quilt top on to the wadding/batting. Gently pull, persuade and cajole until it lies flat and as square as possible; use more pins to anchor it to the carpet. The carpet will not be damaged by this operation, but avoid using any shag pile carpets.

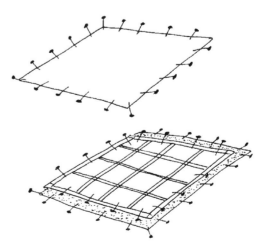

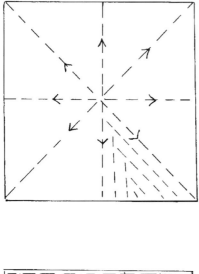

4. Tack the layers together, using a long needle and a contrasting coloured thread (easier to remove afterwards). Commence tacking at the centre and work towards the edge. There are many different ways to tack/baste a quilt; to me it seems logical to work out from the centre easing all the layers simultaneously. (Similar to smoothing the creases from sheets or tablecloths.) I prefer to stitch the eight major bisecting lines first, then systematically fill in each section with parallel lines. Lines approx. 3"/4"(8cm/10cm) apart with the basting 2"/3"(5cm/8cm) long.

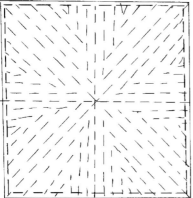

Pushing and pulling the needle through the layers is hard graft: use a very long needle. Some people advise using a teaspoon to help raise the needle. the spoon can be used to depress the layers enabling the needle to slide more easily through. Wear a thimble to prevent sore fingers. Friends are useful for this job - have a 'Tacking up' party - lay on some food and booze but don't serve beans as the crawling about on the floor may be disastrous!

5. Before you pick the quilt off the floor, tack/baste all round the edges. Remove all pins and roughly trim backing material. Chop the excess wadding/batting off *but leave sufficent for the binding*.

## Quilting

The layers have to be anchored together to prevent the pieces flapping about. Quilting solves the problem. It is generally interpreted to mean a form of stitching, but there are other ways to fasten the 'sandwich'.

There must be hundreds of books written solely about quilting. These explain exactly how and where to do it, give patterns and designs that can be stitched and expound upon the mysteries of hand and machine quilting. Try the local quilt/craft shops for more information. Sadly some people get really bothered about quilting and fret if they can't do 'x' amount of stitches to the inch or their machine stitching is uneven. There is no doubt that it is a splendid art form. Go to some of the national exhibitions and see the exquisite work on display, then you will be fired with enthusiasm to learn more. Then view the old antique quilts and be heartened by the quality of some of the stitching - these quilts have stood the test of time and are still usable.

Textured quilts are hard to quilt as there are so many layers. You may prefer to minimise the stitching because of the thickness or alternatively tie the layers.

The tips given here are very rudimentary as this is not a manual on quilting.

**A quilting tie** is probably one of the easiest options. You can make as many or as few as you like but a tie at 6"(15cm) intervals will probably be enough. Quilts need to have sufficient ties to hold the layers securely - if the layers slip around when you think you've finished  do some more. Make the tie from any thread you fancy. Try embroidery silk, buttonhole thread, wool, polyester, silk or a firm cotton.

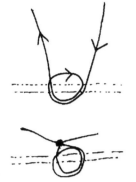

Simply thread a needle; pass through the layers leaving a tail; up to the top and down the first hole; back up again; leave a long end and tie together with a reef knot for preference (right over left and under; left over right and under). Trim the ends where desired, or you could tie a bow. This can be done from top to bottom or vice versa with the ends forming a decorative feature on the R/S or dangling from the underside.

Why not tie the layers including a bead, button, tassel or tiny Suffolk Puff (see Glossary) as you sew? There's no reason why you cannot simply catch the layers together with a small firm stitch. On completion of the ties you must hand-stitch round the outer edges to anchor all the materials together.

**Hand quilting** is also very easy but can be time consuming. Small fine quilting needles (sometimes called betweens) are used and special waxed quilting thread. The thread is waxed to enable it to pull through the layers more easily, if pre-waxed thread is not available, then wax your own with a bar of beeswax (available from quilt stores). Thread can also be 'waxed' with hard soap. You will need thimbles and/or some form of protection for your fingers.

The normal stitch employed for hand quilting is a running stitch, but some people prefer a stab or even backstitch. All knots are meant to be buried within the layers, and the back should look as good as the front although the stitching is often smaller on the underside. *Ideally you should work from the centre out, sewing through all the layers with an even stitch length on both sides - n.b. the lengths are likely to vary*. Designs can be marked either before tacking the quilt together or as you go but do use a removable marking pen or a  sharp H pencil (my favourite).

*Remember - quilting is a way of defining the design, adding texture and anchoring the layers together*.

Relax about the hand quilting. There is such a lot of 'hype' talked about stitch length, quantity of stitches to the inch, etc. For instance, the Japanese style of quilting - Sashiko - displays much larger stitches with a thick gauge thread. Different hands work in different ways and everyone's flexibility varies; you may not be able to manipulate the needle in the same manner as the brilliant quilter who lives next door - that's your story! In addition, there is no doubt that fine, well-washed fabrics quilt more easily than unwashed firm weaves.

Now, I have given you several valid excuses for the quality of your hand-quilting; the only rule is ............

*Keep the stitch lengths and spaces in between as even as possible.*

*Don't forget to sew round the outer edges to anchor the layers together after you have finished the quilting.*

**Machine quilting** is a completely different ballgame to hand quilting. Once again there are many books and even videos on the subject. Use of a walking foot is recommended by many people, but personally I prefer to use a darning/hopper foot and work freely. There are several different styles to select for machine quilting; three of them are -

1. 'Stitch in the Ditch' The 'ditch' is the stitched join (groove) between the pieces. All the stitching is done between the pieces, and the idea is to stay in this groove and not deviate! You are actually sewing through the original stitching of the top of the quilt and the other layers. To quilt a multicoloured sample, match the thread to one of the colours and attempt to limit any meanders on to this fabric. (Use of invisible thread does disguise the mistakes.) Placing your hands gently on either side of the seam and applying gentle pressure to keep it flat may help you to see the join more easily. Maintain a moderate even speed although certain sewing machines cannot be operated this way; it's all or nothing, (this makes it very difficult to control!). Set a longer stitch length as the wadding causes the stitch to contract. When turning a corner, lower the needle into the seam, raise the presser foot and pivot round. Some presser feet are very hard to align as the size of the foot obscures the seam. Finally I have discovered that wearing bifocals does make it awkward to see the seam line - a good excuse!!

2. Topstitching or Echo Quilting is most easily created by using the edge of the presser foot as a guide, and following round the outlines of the shape you wish to delineate. Again use a longer stitch length, drop the needle into the work at the corners and pivot round. Thread choice can add a further dimension to the appearance. But if you are not too confident, use matching threads to the fabric and the deviations from the chosen path will be less obvious.

3. Free Machine Quilting is normally executed by attaching the darning/hopper foot and lowering or covering the feed dogs. Some sewing machines do not have a darning foot but there may be a lever or knob that controls the amount of pressure on the presser foot (see instruction book). By reducing the pressure to zero and using the ordinary presser foot it is possible to free machine quilt, although not as easily as with a darning foot.

This subject has been mentioned in both the last books and is memorable for its alcoholic content. For those who do not possess them here is a reminder:

There is no doubt that practice makes perfect; well, it improves it. This is one of those techniques that need a relaxed operator (glass of wine (or two) recommended before commencing). Push the sewing machine further away than normal. Sit comfortably; lean towards the machine keeping the spine straight, pushing your bottom out and resting your elbows on the table to take the weight. The wrists need to be free and flexible. Relax and drop your shoulders: students with rigid shoulders up under their ears do not perform so well.

So you are sitting correctly, have consumed the vino and have relaxed. You have lowered the feed dogs, attached the darning foot, positioned the work under the needle and all you have to do is construct a series of rounded squiggles. These should not cross over each other nor have points or spikes, but flow evenly over the selected area as in the diagram. Bet the telephone rings!

Try it; *grasp the material firmly*, do not have flat hands. Bring the lower thread to the top surface to prevent it tangling underneath, and hold both ends for the first few stitches. Maintain an even speed as you swing the work in a series of arcs (similar to steering a car). *Relax!*

Using this technique will enhance the textural effect. It is difficult at first but keep experimenting and if you can't achieve the random curves - have spikes!

*Now you too can do it - free machine quilting that is.*

The biggest problem with free machine quilting is the grasping of the work - you really need a steering wheel or something to hang on to. There are horseshoe shaped hoops with handles sold nowadays that sit on the top of the quilt thus giving you something to grasp - it is moved as you complete each section. Years before these came out, I used and still do the inner ring of an 8"(20cm) embroidery hoop. This is placed underneath the quilt (between quilt and machine bed) giving you the 'steering wheel'.

Keep a little tension on the quilt by spreading it firmly over the hoop, stretched and pressed against the needle plate; grasp the rim through the layers and manoeuvre the work as you sew. The neat thing about this little wheeze is that it travels with you as you stitch - once you have completed a section simply shunt the hoop along underneath to the next section and continue. This sounds totally batty but it works - try it and see. Admittedly, the plastic horseshoes have large handles, which are somewhat more convenient for not so nimble hands.

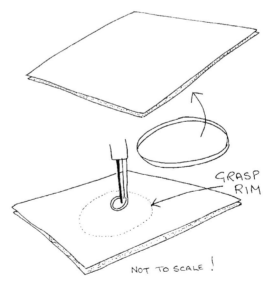

GRASP RIM

NOT TO SCALE !

In addition, some people recommend the special quilting rubber gloves with the raised bubbles on the front, which help in gripping the quilt.

*On completion of any quilting - remember to sew round the entire outer edges to anchor the layers together.*

# Binding

Finally, to complete the masterpiece add the binding. This is the last strip that seals the raw edges on the quilt. Guess what? - there are several ways to apply and make binding. It can be constructed from bias cut fabric or straight strips.

Bias cut fabric is very useful and indeed must be used on any curved edges. It is limited in the usable width (wide bias strips lack the same flexibility as narrow ones) and some people find difficulty with cutting and joining (see page 28). Bias binding may be attached in a continuous strip round all the edges of the quilt and the corners should be mitred. Trim back any surplus wadding/batting to the raw edges of the quilt if employing this technique.

### Bias Binding - ½"(1cm) wide

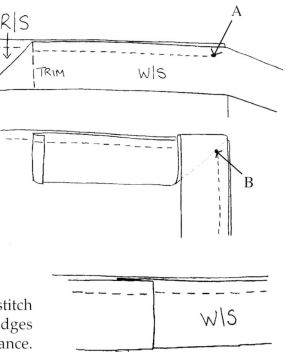

1. Measure the total external dimensions of the quilt. Cut sufficient 1½"(3cm) wide bias strips to fit this length (join if necessary - see page 28). Trim the starting end straight; fold raw edge over. It is easiest to begin somewhere on a straight section, but when you are really used to the technique you will be able to start and stop on a corner.

Put R/S of binding to R/S of quilt; stitch along the seam keeping all raw edges together. Use ¼"(0.5cm) seam allowance. Stop ¼"(0.5cm) from the first corner (**A**).

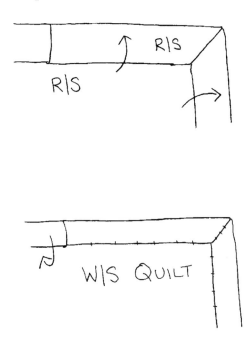

2. *Mitre the bias on the corners* as shown in diagrams by folding strip at right angles to form a triangle. Commence the stitching the other side of triangle at **B**. (**A** and **B** touch either side of the triangle.) Lay the last section over the first; trim to approximately ½"(1cm) past the starting end. Fold over and turn the raw edges to the back. *Carefully measure the depth of the binding on the R/S and pin.* If desired, press the edge gently to retain fold - *don't iron the quilt as any polyester batting/wadding could be damaged.* Turn quilt over, and fold the seam allowance of the binding under; hand slipstitch in place. The mitred corners will fold as in the diagram but may need a jiggle!

## Straight Cut Binding

1. To calculate the cutting sizes, decide on the width of the binding. *Multiply this amount by two, then add seam allowances* to get the correct measurement.

2. Measure the opposite sides of the quilt. Cut sufficient length of strips to this measurement (join if necessary) by the chosen width. Check that both pieces are the same length. Before you attach the strips, consider how much wadding/ batting to leave attached for the binding. A plump and well padded edge is achieved by trimming the surplus wadding to ½"(1cm) less than the binding. This will then be doubled over to make a firmer slightly puffy binding that has greater durability. For a less padded edge, cut to finished width of binding (trim more) and then the edge will be flatter. A single layer of wadding does wear quite thin with the passage of time; personally I prefer the thicker edging.

Stitch strips to the selected sides first, then measure the remaining two sides. Cut strips to match and attach (as in Borders page 88).

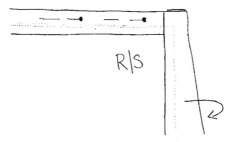

R\S

3. *Work from the R/S of Quilt and measure carefully as you fold* the binding over and pin to the W/S. Make sure that the binding is level and even on the R/S.

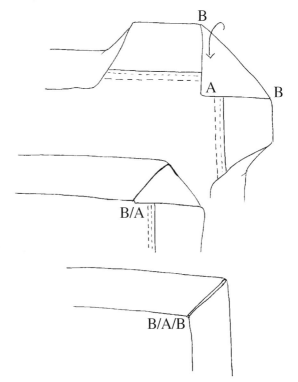

Mitre the corners on the back by turning Quilt to W/S; remove the pins from the corner area; fold corner diagonally to form a triangle; fold over until the point extends beyond the previous stitching by ¼"(0.5cm). **A** is folded over and lies diagonally across the triangle; **B** follows suit as in diagram. **A** and **B** lie side by side. (Some books recommend cutting the corner off to reduce bulk but in my opinion play safe and leave it on.)

4. Finally tuck the seam allowance under on the back. Pin in place before slip stitching the edges to the quilt. Try not to stitch through all the layers as this can show on the R/S. Slip stitch along the mitre for a tidier appearance.

**Relax - you've done it! Well done.**

# Upside Down & Down Under

Sadly, space is at a premium and all the anecdotes cannot be related. As you may have noticed in the foreword I have been and am going again to New Zealand. These days we (royal one) are quite the little globetrotter, teaching in many unusual places. For me travelling is a most enjoyable occupation as you meet such a wide variety of people and have lots of adventures. I started keeping a diary in N.Z. and had every intention of relating the contents in this book, but my apologies - the 'Trials of a Travelling Tucker' will have to wait for book four (unless I write very small). Did you think this was the last? Sorry to disappoint you. The next excursion into print will be either garments and fashion-oriented, or packed with silly notions for decorations or maybe something completely different.

I really liked New Zealand as it is a most beautiful country filled with charming people, excellent fish and chips and gorgeous dog handlers at the airport (male naturally). The only drawbacks are that you can't buy a bottle of wine on Sundays very easily and the drains in Rotorua need serious attention. (No one told me that they have sulphur springs and the pong is all pervading.) Now I know why, and when I saw my first ever bubbling and boiling mud pool it was love at first sight. Some people do get turned on by the strangest things!

Despite being footloose and fancy free in N.Z. I failed abysmally to collect any interesting guys, but I did get an interesting view of several of them. Walking through the suburbs of Auckland I came across a party of young men. They were cavorting on the lawn outside their house, dressed in bathing costumes, silly wigs, false beards, makeup and not a lot else. Fascinated by the sight, I whipped out the camera and prepared to take a picture. I was spotted. To my horror, they promptly turned round, dropped everything and I had a lovely vista of round pink bottoms. Naturally I took the picture, thanked them for their kindness and proceeded on my way, hoping they would not see the blushes. Did I really want to return from my walk the same way? What else might I have seen? The mind boggles!

In addition to keeping a diary, I felt that I would like a visual memento of the trip and persuaded all the store owners to give me a quarter of fabric. This material had to represent some thought, feeling or colour that they felt was reminiscent of New Zealand. The quilt is pictured opposite page 95 and just sort of happened. It is a collection of some of the textural qualities that will always remind me of this country. The stores that I would like to thank are:

Bernina Sewing Centre, Whangarei.          Cottage Flair, Rotorua.
Still Quilting, New Plymouth.               Village Books & Crafts, Palmerston Nth
Quilt Connection, Wellington.              Creations Unlimited, Nelson.
The Looking Class, Picton.                 Elna Sewing Centre, Christchurch.
Patchwork Barn, Birkenhead.                The Quilt Shop, Freemans Bay.
Stitch & Craft, Hunters Corner.            Margaret Barrett Distributors, Auckland

(Full names and addresses are available from MBD - see International Distributors - page 112)

# The Fourth Man

I met 23 different gentlemen in the course of four months or so. Each chap was pleasant enough but none of them really clicked. I was beginning to get tired of writing letters, trotting off on yet another blind date, and ploughing my way through yet another meal, and I almost felt that being single had a lot to offer. My mother persuaded me to have one last go at the 'Times'. I suspect that she enjoyed hearing the tales of my adventures and would have missed the telephone calls, "Mother, you should have seen the guy last night. He wore a yellow woolly that his Grannie knitted, with baggy trousers, hung his hankie on his belt because it might spoil the line of his trousers. (I couldn't understand this as they fitted him so badly). Guess what! His car had furry dice etc. etc."

The letter that caught my eye said: *"Desperately seeking simple fun loving lover and companion for 40 something, reasonably fit, separated, financially secure, n/s, 6' 1"human. Into skiing, squash, old cars, cooking, concerts, travel etc. High powered intellectuals, workaholics & flautists need not apply. Hants/Sussex Border."*

This was just my kind of man. Being a simple soul who is not intellectual nor a workaholic, likes concerts, travel and cooking, I would fit the bill exactly. (Can't we delude ourselves when necessary!) In addition to the usual letter, I replied: *"Firstly, I am unable to play the flaut, I can blow my own trumpet, the recorder occasionally and can even tinkle on the piano. Secondly, I adore squashing into old cars. Thirdly, do you think that running and cycling could substitute for skiing? I'm good at going downhill but up hill leaves me breathless hence the inability to play the flaut!"*

He liked the letter and wrote back with the information that he disliked blackcurrant jam, television soaps and Virginia Bottomley. In addition, he wrote books from the semi-historical to bonkerama. Gosh, another writer! Obviously not to be missed; I rang him up. We agreed to meet at the Happy Eater on the A3. I arrived early, parked the car advantageously so that I could see the other cars arriving. If he looked dreadful, then I could leave quickly. His car arrived and he seemed, on first glance to be acceptable and I stayed. In the back of his estate was a spendid golden retriever. To my amazement, he got out of the car, raised the tailgate and the dog just sat there. The dog remained happily sitting in the car the entire time we talked and had coffee. I was most impressed. We chatted. He was definitely OK. The dog was even better. In fact they looked a bit alike, both having red-gold hair and beards.

He foolishly offered to proof read my book. I was overjoyed. I could spin the proof reading out for ages and who knows what might happen? Having finished the coffee, I was allowed to meet the hound. Splendid animal. If his master was as nice as the dog ........

It is now four years on. Sadly the dog has gone to higher climes but his master remains. Neither of us buys the "Times" any more.

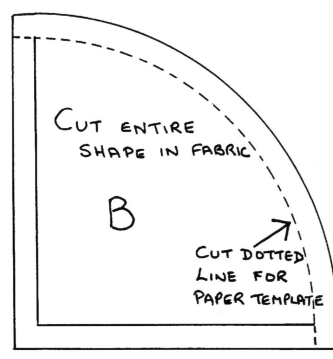

CUT ENTIRE SHAPE IN FABRIC

B

CUT DOTTED LINE FOR PAPER TEMPLATE

## Templates for Tucked Up Fan - Page 52

*Be very careful if photocopying the templates. Check it is an exact replica of the templates. Not all photocopiers are absolutely accurate in their reproduction. Tracing is probably the best option.*

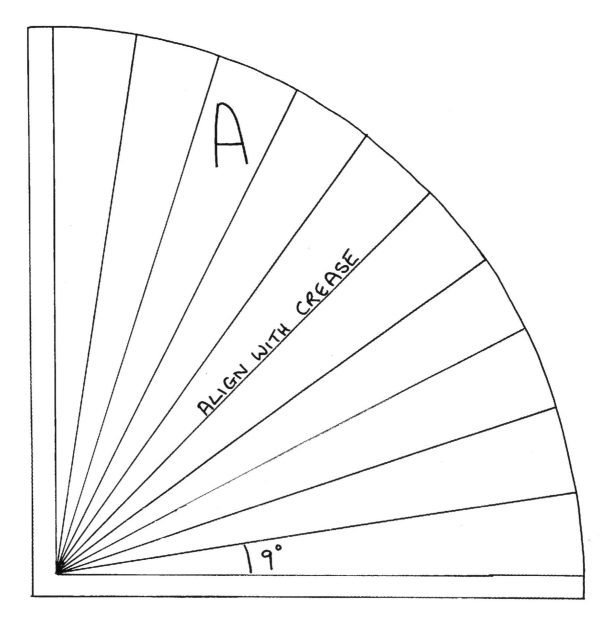

A

ALIGN WITH CREASE

9°

# Shops & Suppliers

(Random selection of locations.)

*Austin Sykes
74/77 St. Pancras, Chichester,
West Sussex
Tel: 01243 782139

*The Bramble Patch
West Street, Weedon
Northants NN7 4QU
Tel: 01327 342212

Campden Quilters Patch,
Blacksmith House,
High Street,
Chipping Campden GL55 6AT
Tel: 01386 840181

Calico Threads
Boreland park, Kirn
Dunoon, Argyll PA23 8HF
Tel: 01369 703007

*The Cotton Patch
1285 Stratford Road, Hall Green
Birmingham B28 9AJ
Tel: 0121 7022840
Fax: 0121 7785924

*Country Crafts
10a St. Mary's Walk
Hailsham, East Sussex
Tel: 01323 442271

*Country Threads
2 Pierrepoint Place
Bath BA1 1JX
Tel: 01225 480056

*Creative Quilting
3 Bridge Road, Hampton Court
Surrey KT8 9EU
Tel: 0181 941 7075

**(Rulers, mats and rotary cutters)**
Creative Grids
77 Westfield Road
Leicester LE3 6HU
Tel/Fax: 0116 2857151

Doughty's Quilt Shop
3 Capuchin Yard
Hereford HR1 2LR
01432 267542

*Embsay Mills
Embsay
Skipton, North Yorks
Tel: 01756 700946

Fourshire Books
17 High Street,
Moreton-in-the-Marsh
Gloucs GL56 0AF
Tel: 01608 651451

Green Hill
27 Bell Street, Romsey
Hampshire SO51 8GY
Tel: 01794 517973

Manifold Valley Patchwork
Unit 2, Buxton Road, Lognor
Buxton, SK17 0NZ
Tel: 01298 83801

*Missenden Abbey
**(Teaching only)**
Great Missenden,
Bucks HP16 0BD
Tel: 01494 862904

Moor Silks & Yarns
Paddons Row, Brook Street
Tavistock, Devon PL19 0HF
Tel: 01822 612624

*Needle & Thread
80 High Street, Horsell
Woking, Surrey GU21 4SZ
Tel: 01483 762995

*Needlepatch
Mangerton Mill, Mangerton
Bridport, Dorset DT6 3SG
Tel: 01308 485689

Patchwork House
2/3 Charlecombe Court, Stoke Lane
Westbury-on-Trym, Bristol BS9 3RL
Tel: 0117 907991   Fax: 0117 9079992

Patchworkers Paradise
16 East Street, Blandford Forum
Dorset DTII 7DR
Tel: 01258 456099

Patchwork Plus
129 Station Road, Cark-in-
Cartmel
Grange-over-Sands,
Cumbria LA11 7NY
Tel: 01539 559009

**(Calico supplier)**
Pick 'n Choose
56 Station Road, Northwich
Cheshire CW9 5RB
Tel: 01606 415523
Fax: 01606 47255

*Purely Patchwork
23 High Street, Linlithgow
Scotland EH49 7AB
Tel/Fax: 01506 846200

Quilters Cottage
60 Bridge Street, Garstang
Preston, Lancs PR3 1YB
Tel: 01995 603929

*Quilt Basics
Unit 19, Chiltern House,
Waterside, Chesham,
Bucks HP5 1PS
Tel: 01494 791401
Fax: 01494 785202

*Quilters Haven
68 High Street,
Wickham Market
Suffolk IP13 0QU
Tel: 01728 746275

*The Quilt Room
20 West Street, Dorking
Surrey RH4 1BL
Tel: 01306 740739
Fax: 01306 877407

*Red Cottage Crafts
1 Rawdon Court, Main Street,
Moira, Co. Armagh BT67 0LQ
Tel: 01846 619172

*West Dean College **(Teaching only)**
West Dean, Chichester
West Sussex PO18 0QZ
Tel: 01243 811301

*Village Fabrics
4/5 St. Leonards Square, Wallingford,
Oxon OX10 0AS
Tel: 01491 204100
Fax: 01491 204013

## International Distributors

Quilter's Resources Inc.
P.O. Box 148850, Chicago,
Illinois 60614, U.S.A.
Tel: 773 278 5695
Fax: 773 278 1348

Margaret Barrett Distributors Ltd.
19 Beasley Avenue,
P.O. Box 12-034, Penrose,
Auckland, New Zealand
Tel: 64-9-525 6142
Fax: 64-9-525 6382

---

*Jennie Rayment Workshops*

# Jennie Rayment

To book for workshops or lectures,
please contact:

5 Queen Street
Emsworth
Hampshire
PO10 7BJ
Tel/Fax: 01243 374860
E-mail jenrayment@aol.com

Classes, talks, show & tell,
demonstrations can be arranged to
suit.

It is advisable to book early and all
engagements must be in writing.
Jennie is happy to travel worldwide if
requested.

# Glossary

**Backing**: The fabric used underneath a sample or the underside of a cushion or quilt.

**Baltimore Rosebud**: Folded square designed to resemble a petal often used in appliqué.

**Baste**: Securing of layers with a long stitch to prevent movement.

**Batting**: Wadding or filling frequently made from polyester or cotton fibres used in between or underneath fabric for quilting purposes.

**Bias**: Diagonal of the woven grain (45 degrees to the selvedge).

**Borders**: Fabric attached to the outer edges to frame the article.

**Broderie anglais**: Openwork embroidery frequently made in pure cotton fabric.

**Calico**: **(British definition.)** Plain woven strong cotton cloth (sometimes bleached) with a distinctive fleck in the weave. A loomstate cloth woven from pure natural thread.

**Catch**: Several small stitches in the same place for securing an edge/corner of material.

**Cathedral Window Patchwork**: Traditional design constructed from folded and stitched squares.

**Chintz**: Close-weave shiny cotton cloth with a resin coating for that characteristic sheen.

**Colour Wheel**: All the colours of the spectrum (red, orange, yellow, green, blue, indigo, violet) arranged as segments of a circle.

**Cretonne**: A washable hard-wearing fabric similar to unglazed chintz; liable to shrink.

**Grain**: Direction of the weave. Weft fibres run across from selvedge to selvedge; warp fibres are parallel to the selvedge.

**Log Cabin Patchwork**: Traditional designs made from strips of material frequently laid out in a square format. The square is often divided diagonally into light and dark colours.

**Mercerised Cotton**: Treated to both strengthen and have a silky sheen.

**Muslin**: Fine soft cotton fabric resembling gauze in appearance. **(British definition.)**

**Vilene**: Interfacing/stabiliser made from bonded fibres. comes in different thicknesses.

**Pin Tucks**: Fine tucks sometimes enclosing a cord.

**Pinwheel**: Rotation of one shape at 90° round a central point.

**Prairie Points**: Squares folded into quarter triangles.

**R/S**: Right side of material.

**Ruche/Ruching**: Gathered material often in a strip, used for decorative effect.

**Satin Stitch**: The stitch effect produced by increasing the stitch width and decreasing the stitch length of the zig-zag stitch on the sewing machine.

**S/A or Seam Allowance**: Distance between the stitch line and the edge of the fabric.

**Selvedge/selvage**: The firm edges of the fabric running parallel to the warp threads.

**Somerset/Folded Squares**: Squares folded into rectangles then into triangles.

**Sharkstooth**: USA term for Somerset/Folded square patches.

**Sharon Square**: Particular method of folding a square.

**Stay stitching**: Securing of layers with a long stitch to prevent movement.

**Suffolk Puff**: Small circle of tightly gathered fabric someimes called a YoYo.

**Tack**: **(British Definition)**: Securing of layers with a long stitch to prevent movement **(USA Definition)**: small securing stitch in one place.

**W/S**: Wrong or underside of fabric.

**Wadding**: Batting or filling frequently made from polyester or cotton fibres used in between or underneath fabric for quilting purposes.

# Index